RESTORIED®

A BLUEPRINT TO TRANSFORM YOUR LIFE & REWRITE YOUR STORY

FROM QUEENS GIRL TO KINGDOM WARRIOR

DANIELLE URSINI

This book was printed in the United States of America.

To order additional copies of this book or to schedule speaking engagements, contact:

Danielle Ursini, LLC
South Florida
(561) 358-0318
danielle@restoried.net

www.restoried.net

DEDICATION

To my brother, John, who carried me in his arms as a newborn and on his shoulders throughout my childhood. Your unwavering love, support, and protection gave me the strength to persevere. It was a privilege and honor carrying you until you took your last breath.

To my children, Erik & Alexandra, whom I carried for a momentary season, yet you have been my unceasing inspiration to carry on and press forward. I'm so proud of you both and truly honored to be your mom.

TABLE OF CONTENTS

FOREWORD

I was a TV news journalist in South Florida for 26-years and met Danielle when her husband became a supporter of the Angels of Charity, a Palm Beach fundraising group that raised millions of dollars for local organizations, of which I was a member. Like Danielle, the Angels and many investors, I was duped by her husband's charismatic personality, perceived financial prowess and generous charitable promises. None of us knew his monumental success was being tenuously supported by lies, games of manipulation and emotional betrayal.. all for personal gain.

It surprised me that Danielle, a licensed mental health professional could be misled, but having read "ReStoried," I now realize how easily we can all fall victim to such masters of deception. You are likely to connect with her story on many levels, from a dysfunctional family to divorce and caregiving. What makes this book unique is that she puts a face on and defines many of our daily struggles, using her own life as an illustration and then offering a therapist's insight as to next steps. It's as though she took herself on as a client.

Perhaps the most valuable lesson that comes from "ReStoried" is Danielle's message of healing. That out of tremendous pain, heartache and unfathomable challenges, one can come to a place of peace, contentment and purpose. I share her belief that such a place can only be found in the arms of a loving God, through His supernatural strength and by the teachings of His Son, Jesus Christ. I pray readers are touched by her vulnerability, embrace the tools she offers to cope with life's frequent mysteries and are led to the one true Healer.

Chandra Bill-Rabenecker
Former TV news journalist, member of The Angels of Charity

ABOUT RESTORIED®

ReStoried®. Not a typo. Not restored. One definition of "restored" is "to give something previously stolen, taken away, or lost back to the original owner or recipient." Although, like many of you, I feel that much has been stolen or taken away throughout my life, the intangible, emotional, and relational losses cannot be given back. Reflecting on my childhood, I believe I was robbed of a sense of safety, security, trust, peace, and innocence. In adulthood, I was deprived of a healthy, lifelong marriage, my protective older brother, friendships, peace, and pure joy. I don't believe these things can be restored, but perhaps they can be replaced.

Another definition of "restored" is "to return someone to a former condition, place, or position." Honestly, I have no desire to return to a previous condition, place, or position in my life. My character as a teenager and young adult had many flaws—rebellious, deceptive, and selfish—to name a few. Through my newfound faith at age 30, my character flaws were acknowledged, confessed, and gradually replaced with growing obedience, honesty, and humility. These traits were characteristic of my early childhood personality, so some restoration in fact occurred.

Now, 25 years later, I'm visiting my son in San Diego, California. I wake up in my room at the Coronado Bay Resort and make myself a cup of green tea. Sitting down with my Gratitude Journal, I list all that I am grateful for today. When asked to write down a "word of the day," I choose the word "restored." This week away from my home in Florida, my counseling practice, and my informal counseling of family and friends truly feels like restoration. On this crisp 68-degree July morning, I decided to head to the beach for my walk. On the way, I notice a display board and am intrigued that the word staring at me across the top is "Restoration," referring to the Salt Pond Restoration Project. My word of the day is right there on the display board.

On this same trip, I was reading a book in which the author explored her experiences as a therapist and a client. She explained that therapy is a process of understanding oneself and letting go of the limiting stories one has told oneself about who they are. From my practice and personal life, I have learned that we become trapped in the stories we've told ourselves about ourselves from early childhood to the present. These limiting stories include themes such as: *"I'm not good enough," "I don't matter," "I was not wanted," and "It was my fault."* Therapy helps us rewrite our story, changing the theme to be more self-affirming and allowing us a new freedom to live life abundantly.

As I continued my morning walk, two Christian songs came to mind. Both refer to God rewriting our story. In the first song, "Till I Found You," Phil Wickham sings, "I searched through the Earth for something that could satisfy" and "A peace for the hurt I had buried deep inside." Only through his faith in God does he discover, "I finally found that everything I needed was always right in front of me . . . You're rewriting my story, and I'm brand new like a morning."

In the second song, "God's Not Done with You," Tauren Wells writes,

> He's got a plan. . .
> He's gonna finish what He started . . .
> He's not done
> God's not done writing your story.

I began to realize that through my own therapy experience, as well as through my faith in God, the limiting stories that I was trapped in for many years were rewritten over time. God rewrote my story. He not only restored me— He Re-Storied me!

The Engagement

For the past 20 years, I've been trapped in a story that replays over and over in my mind. It's time for a new story. Time to be Re-Storied. But first, I will narrate the old story for the final time, forgive all who have left scars, and forgive myself in order for the new story to be written.

My profession and calling for the past 35 years have been as a counselor. As I tell my story, you will notice flag icons. These icons represent "red flags" or warning signs that there is a problem that needs to be noticed and addressed in a relationship. Unfortunately, red flags are often ignored, especially in new relationships. You will also notice couch icons throughout my story. These sections labeled "couch to couch," are found at the end of chapters. They are lessons learned as a client on my own therapist's couch, as well as sitting in the therapist chair and learning from my clients. I hope that sharing all of these insights and practical applications as you sit on your couch at home will save you from years of therapy.

In March 1993, I was a 28-year-old single woman who resorted to the classifieds to meet my future husband, Bob (not his real name). My roommate was meeting men through this "social media" platform, and although I resisted for many months—convinced I would meet a serial killer—I picked up the landline, dialed the toll-free number, and listened to two profiles. One called me back, and we spoke for three hours.

Bob truly seemed like my perfect match. We had the same birthday, our mothers both had sisters named "Dolores," and we both had master's degrees. Bob stated that he had two master's degrees, one of which was from the University of Miami, where he also played football.

In that first phone conversation, he also told me that he had created the Marvel character Wolverine and that he was a stockbroker. When we finished the phone call, my roommate was eager to hear all about him. I asked her what a stockbroker was, who Wolverine was, and if the University of Miami had a good football team. She informed me that UM had won several national championships.

On our first date, we met at his ocean-view office and then went to see the movie *Aladdin*. I was 28, and he was 30. We were both young professionals who wanted to be married and have a family. Like Aladdin, Bob would show me "a whole new world."

For our mutual birthday in July, we planned a trip to New York to meet my family and friends. I was born and raised in Queens and moved to Florida at the age of 26. My family was eager to meet this "knight in shining armor," as my mother called him. My aunt and uncle, my best friend, and my roommate all booked the same flight to travel with us.

Just prior to boarding, we were delighted to be upgraded to first class. When the captain finished his mid-flight announcements, I was incredibly surprised to hear him include Bob's marriage proposal over the intercom. Bob presented me with the engagement ring, the whole plane cheered, and we were served champagne to celebrate. We were engaged only four months after we met—too much, too soon. 🏴

We had a formal engagement party at an exclusive Italian restaurant in Queens. It was a known Mafia-owned establishment which my father frequented. My father worked in construction in Queens and was "connected." I would find out 20 years later that my father introduced Bob to these men, hoping that his future son-in-law could shelter their money in offshore accounts. I will share more about my father and the Mob later in my story.

When we returned to Florida, we had another engagement party at Bob's office to celebrate with our local family and friends. After the party, we all went to a dance club.

One of Bob's friends was too intoxicated to drive home at 1:00 AM, so Bob handed me the keys to his Jaguar to drive behind them. Little did I know, Jaguars have two gas tanks, and both were empty. Bob took off in his friend's car, and I was left alone to figure out where the gas tanks were and how to fill them. We didn't yet have cellphones, so I couldn't call him. I arrived at his house at 2:30 AM. I don't recall an apology or taking ownership of leaving his young fiancée alone and unprotected in the middle of the night. ◣

When I first met Bob, he had just opened his office. I purchased a beautiful birds of paradise plant arrangement to acknowledge his Grand Opening. During our engagement, I opened my private practice in an adjoining office to his. He surprised me with a remarkably similar plant arrangement to celebrate my new endeavor. I was deeply moved by his thoughtfulness.

Unfortunately, the celebration bubble quickly burst. My best friend insisted that she had ordered that plant arrangement and had it delivered to the office. She confirmed delivery with the florist and confronted Bob with the receipt, but he insisted that he purchased the same arrangement. She believed he received the delivery and removed her note card before bringing it to me. ◣

I found myself in a difficult position between my best friend and my fiancé. My friend would later very lovingly tell

4

me—before and on my wedding day—that she thought I was making the worst mistake of my life. 🏴

She was right about the marriage, except that I have an amazing son and daughter, and I would go through it all again just to be their mom.

In the months before the wedding, I wanted to make a scrapbook for Bob of all his accomplishments throughout his childhood and into adulthood. I asked for his degrees and pictures of him playing football for the University of Miami. He told me that he had lived in a mobile home, and there was a house fire. He lost his degrees and all his pictures. The empath in me was triggered, and I felt so sad for him. I asked if he tried to obtain duplicate copies of his degrees and football photos from UM. I even offered to take on this mission, but he avoided my questions and discouraged pursuing these lost items. 🏴

In regard to being the creator of Wolverine, this was the story he would tell. He entered and won an art contest in elementary school. The prize was to intern with Jim Davis, the creator of Garfield. Prior to winning the contest, he had submitted Wolverine to Marvel Comics. He recalls looking through a comic book in the grocery store and seeing his character with the Hulk. He informed Jim Davis, who then contacted Marvel Comics and advocated for him. Unfortunately, the character was not copyrighted, and Marvel would not acknowledge Bob as the creator. Instead, they offered him a collection of comic books. The empath in me was once again triggered, and I felt so sad for him that his Wolverine character was stolen by Marvel Comics. ⚑

And so, we continued planning our wedding for April 1994 and having our first home built in Wellington. We were planning a dream wedding and having a dream home built in a community called Emerald Forest. The name always reminded me of the Emerald City in the Wizard of Oz. Sadly, my husband would turn out to be a "master of illusion" just like the Wonderful Wizard of Oz. Before I could see behind the screen, I was taken up in a whirlwind of planning our wedding, decorating our new home, and dreaming of a honeymoon in Maui, Hawaii.

My extended family in New York was not willing to come to Florida for our wedding, so we cancelled the contract with the venue and planned an intimate wedding on the lake across from our new house. My mother planned a second, more formal wedding for family and friends in New York one week later. I would not recommend two weddings in order to accommodate family, but back then, I was not yet versed in healthy boundaries.

For our honeymoon, we stayed at the Grand Wailea, where the movie "Just Go With It" starring Jennifer Aniston and Adam Sandler was filmed. I remember wondering if it would turn out to be a rundown hotel since our stay was complimentary. We checked in and were escorted to the Presidential Suite with a silver sushi boat and champagne awaiting us. The Grand Wailea was actually a 5-star Waldorf Astoria luxury beachfront resort. Our week's stay was comped because Bob guaranteed a company return trip. Years later, I found out that he had misrepresented himself as being from a large corporation with the same last name.

In fact, we did return to the Grand Wailea in December 1997 with a group of 32 business associates, clients, and friends. Everything Bob planned was extravagant. On that trip, we hosted three privately catered dinners in our suite for our guests. He also gathered the group in the on-site chapel, gave a speech about marriage, and presented me with an exquisite 5-carat diamond ring. It sounds like a fairytale and looked like one too.

Couch to Couch: There is this unspoken expectation that women tend to put on themselves—and society reinforces—that we must be married and start a family by 30 years old. Sadly, many women will ignore all red flags and often compromise just to fulfill that expectation.

When you're romantically attracted to another person, your brain releases dopamine, serotonin levels increase, and oxytocin is produced. Dopamine and serotonin are often referred to as "happy hormones," and oxytocin is labeled the "love hormone." Research shows that oxytocin diminishes the capacity to think clearly and reason and can cause forgetfulness.

Practical Application: It is therefore particularly important to introduce your person to family and friends early in a new relationship. Be willing to ask for their impressions and any concerns they may have. Give thoughtful consideration to concerns and red flags they have observed.

The Honeymoon

Our honeymoon in Maui at the Grand Wailea was a dream vacation. The resort and guest services were extraordinary. In addition to our amazing Presidential Suite, we enjoyed the on-site waterpark, in-pool elevator to the top of the water slide, and a 10-foot-deep dive pool to learn the basics of scuba diving.

Bob was a certified diver, but I was not, so I took the class offered at the resort. The instructor highlighted the skill of retrieving your regulator if somehow it falls out of your mouth. I practiced that skill as well as all the other required skills; then, the instructor took a group of us out for a dive. We walked along the shoreline away from the resort and into the ocean about 20 feet deep. Each diver had a buddy, and of course, Bob was mine.

As we began swimming further out and deeper, someone's fin kicked the regulator out of my mouth. I attempted to retrieve my regulator, as I had practiced in class, but I could not find it. The regulator floated away, and I couldn't reach the hose it was attached to. You're not able to make noise underwater, so I couldn't get the attention of Bob, the instructor, or any of the other divers. In fact, when I looked for my husband, the instructor, or the rest of the group, I couldn't find anyone. They had all continued swimming on, leaving me behind with only one remaining choice: to hold my breath, remain calm, and ascend as slowly as possible to avoid decompression sickness, or "the bends." That's exactly what I did. When I reached the surface, I looked around and realized I was too far from the shoreline or the resort to call out for help. There were no boats in sight. So, I just waited for Bob to realize I was missing and come find me.

I definitely dissociated, which helped me cope with the thought that I could have died and been found at the bottom of the ocean. I floated alone on the surface for what felt like an eternity with no people or boats in sight. I'm not even sure if I considered the danger of sharks or other sea creatures. I believe that God protected me from physical harm and from dying. I also believe that God gives our bodies and minds the ability to dissociate in order to survive trauma and then the ability to block these memories until we are able to face them and heal from them.

Bob did find me and seemed more annoyed than concerned for my well-being. I confronted him about this incident 17 years later when I brought our teenagers to visit him in prison in Arkansas. I'll come back to the prison part later. He recalled that I was missing for about 20 minutes and was annoyed that I hadn't stayed with the group. He thought I was right next to him the whole time. This was very traumatic for me, especially since we were on our honeymoon. Once again, he was not concerned for my safety or well-being.

Unfortunately, I didn't yet know God as I do now, nor did I even recall this incident until many years later. I was watching a "Dateline" episode where a couple went scuba diving on their honeymoon. The husband came to the surface without his new bride and informed the other couple on the boat that she was on the bottom of the ocean. When they rescued her, she was already dead. That was the moment that my scuba incident came to mind, and the thought that I could have died. The husband in the episode was later found guilty of removing her regulator and causing her death. I may never know who really kicked the regulator out of my mouth and why my husband was not close to my side as a new diver and his new bride.

Couch to Couch: Dissociation is an involuntary survival mechanism, often triggered by trauma, where your cognitive processes and emotional reactions separate from your body—a "mental escape" when you are not able to physically escape and find safety.

Practical Application: Grounding techniques are highly effective to manage and reduce dissociation. By implementing these practical steps, you will foster a sense of grounding and safety:

- ❖ Practice deep diaphragmatic breathing.
- ❖ Plant your bare feet firmly on the ground.
- ❖ Feel the texture of an object or the chair you're sitting in.
- ❖ Focus on mindfulness to increase your awareness in the present moment.
- ❖ Reconnect your mind with your body through physical activities like dance, Pilates, and stretching.

Extravagant Purchases

We lived in our new Emerald Forest home for one year, during which time we found out I was pregnant with our first child - a son. We were both ecstatic and extremely grateful. My gynecologist had informed me that conception would be difficult due to post-surgery scar tissue. We considered this pregnancy a miracle.

Within two years, I was pregnant with our second child – a daughter, and yet another miracle. The privilege of being mom to my two children has truly been my greatest blessing.

During my first pregnancy, Bob planned for us to visit his clients who were an older retired couple. Bob told them he was a family man, which was especially important to the couple. The only problem was that he had met them years before we were married and told them he already had two children. This was the conversation we had on the way to their home. I was obviously pregnant and would have to lie about this being our third child. I was totally blindsided and refused to lie to them, so I remained silent for most of the evening.

Bob wanted to move into a larger home. He found a home for sale in the Aero Club, which has its own runway for the residents' privately owned planes. We purchased the home, although the mortgage was in my name since he had "credit issues." I also opened his business American Express account in my name for the same reasons. Bob managed all of the finances, paid all of the bills, and filed our income taxes separately (which later turned out to be a blessing). I never knew what his income was, and I was quite surprised when we were in the car one day, and he referred to himself as a "self-made millionaire." ▶

Bob had the house completely gutted and renovated. He was an artist and could have been an interior designer. He furnished and decorated the house exquisitely. Bob displayed his extensive sports memorabilia collection on the walls around the pool table, arcade racing games, and bar area. He also worked with a landscaper and designed all the landscaping.

He had the pool drained and tiled with a green and orange "U" for the University of Miami at the bottom. During one of my trips to New York to visit family, he began constructing a 1,500-square-foot addition behind the house and off the screened-in pool area. The addition would house a home theater with surround sound, a motorized projector screen, four televisions to watch several football games simultaneously, and two levels of seating. There was also a workout room with a full-sized wrestling mat, an office with Marvel collectibles and an extensive comic book collection.

There was a detached garage in addition to the attached garage. Bob had a checkered floor installed in the detached garage, which housed his completely restored '55 Chevy truck, along with his Ferrari, which he later traded in for a Lamborghini. The built-on addition, the Ferrari, and the Lamborghini were never discussed . Bob managed the finances, so he made whatever purchases he wanted. With each large purchase, I would receive a gift of expensive jewelry.

Our close friends lived on the next block. The husband was a pilot. Bob eventually purchased a 6-seater plane and built a hangar on their property. The husband became his personal pilot. We would walk across the lawn to our neighbors and take off on our plane right from the neighborhood runway. The purchase of the plane and the building of the hangar were also not discussed.

Bob also purchased a race car with his company logo on the front hood. He built a mechanic garage on another friend's property. That friend serviced the car and transported it to the raceway.

When our son was about 5 months old, Bob decided to take the Chevy truck out for a ride on a Saturday afternoon. I received a phone call from a Palm Beach County Sheriff informing me that Bob had been arrested and was taken to the county jail. I would need $2000 cash to bail him out. Back then, ATMs had limits on the amount you could withdraw, and banks were already closed for the weekend. I called his attorney, his best friend, and a church friend. We were able to obtain the bail money, and we all went to the county jail. We were there for many hours waiting. When he was finally released, he was furious with his attorney for "not taking care of the check issue" which led to a warrant for his arrest. He never acknowledged nor thanked any of us for obtaining the cash to bail him out and waiting for hours at the jail for him to be released. He also never fully explained the "check issue" that led to the warrant for his arrest. ◥

Couch to Couch: In my many years as a therapist, I have seen a repeated pattern in marriages of husbands buying wives extravagant gifts when they are making unilateral purchases or hiding infidelity, illegal, or immoral behaviors.

Practical Application: Before a couple marries, important topics such as finances should be openly discussed with full disclosure of debt, credit issues, and legal matters. All major decisions, especially major purchases, should be discussed beforehand. Unilateral decisions in a marriage tend to lead to conflict.

Palm Beach Life

We were members of two exclusive private Palm Beach clubs, The Governors Club and The Mar-a-Lago Club. Membership in these private clubs allowed him access to potential wealthy clients and philanthropists. Bob had formed a non-profit charitable foundation for local children's organizations. His foundation, along with the Angels of Charity—a group of women philanthropists—planned elaborate events at Saks Fifth Avenue, Mar-a-Lago Club, Trump Golf Course, the Breakers, and other Palm Beach and Miami venues.

We attended private concerts at Mar-a-Lago, such as the Beach Boys and Kenny G. One evening, Rod Stewart was waiting outside of the restroom lounge for his model wife. Another evening, Whitney Houston was standing next to me at the poolside bar. Of course, we met Donald Trump and both of his ex-wives, Ivana and Marla.

At one of the black-tie charitable events that Bob hosted, I was seated next to the actor Dave Coulier, who played Joey on "Full House." At another event of Bob's, we sat at the table with Mohammed Ali, his wife, and his coach, Al Dundee. We met the astronaut Buzz Aldrin at a charitable event held at the local science museum. We attended an event at the home of Julio Iglesias on Star Island in Miami. I remember walking through the main entrance where there was a grand piano and a child-size grand piano which was for Enrique Iglesias. We also attended several events with local celebrities, such as the Rice brothers, who are twin little people.

We were members of the Golden Canes Society at the University of Miami and made generous donations to the athletic program. We had pre-game access to the luxury suite, and preferential seating during games, and we traveled with the team by plane to away games.

Bob enjoyed a very extravagant lifestyle with access to and admiration from the rich and famous. I admit meeting celebrities and experiencing gourmet dining in exquisite venues was enjoyable. My inner introvert preferred to stay home with our children. I was very tired as a new mom, so I did not look forward to getting ready for these elaborate events or staying out late. I often felt like Julia Roberts in "Pretty Woman," where she required a beauty and wardrobe makeover, as well as etiquette lessons. Honestly, I don't miss the high society lifestyle. I am much more content with fewer material things and more authentic relationships.

Couch to Couch: Narcissistic Personality Disorder involves a pattern of self-centered, arrogant thinking and behavior, lack of empathy and consideration for others, and an excessive need for admiration. Narcissistic men are often drawn to highly empathetic women, focused on his needs and wants, and putting him on the pedestal he desires to live on. Marital conflict usually focuses on his unmet needs, disregard for her needs, lack of attention due to children's needs being addressed, confronting and exposing lies, and being knocked off the pedestal.

Practical Application: Relationships with narcissistic partners or family members can be extremely challenging. Here are basic tips to help protect your mental and physical health, as well as your emotional and spiritual well-being:

- ❖ **Educate Yourself**: Learn about narcissistic personality disorder to better understand your loved ones behavior and develop effective coping strategies. There are many books, articles, and videos on this topic.
- ❖ **Set Boundaries**: Establish clear boundaries to protect your physical and emotional well-being. Be consistent and firm in enforcing them.
- ❖ **Focus on What You Can Control**: Accept that you cannot change your loved one's personality, but you can control how you respond to their behavior.
- ❖ **Choose Your Battles Wisely**: Recognize when to confront important issues and when to step back. Use "I" statements to express your feelings without blaming or criticizing. This can help reduce defensiveness and open up more constructive dialogue.
- ❖ **Build Your Support System**: Connect with friends, family, or a support group who understand your situation and can offer wise counsel and encouragement.
- ❖ **Develop a Safety Plan**: If the relationship becomes abusive, have a safety plan in place. Know where you can go and whom you can contact for help.

Newfound Faith

When Bob and I met, our faith backgrounds were similar. We were both raised Catholic more by tradition than in practice. I was born into an Italian Catholic family in Queens, New York. I attended a Christian kindergarten, then a Catholic elementary school, high school, and college. At 16 years old, my first job was in a Jewish bakery owned by an Italian baker. I only knew Catholic churches and Jewish synagogues, so I had no idea that there were numerous Christian denominations until I moved to Florida as a young adult.

For most of those young adult years, I was estranged from the church and from God. Bob was attending a non-denominational church, which I was not familiar with. I'm grateful that he introduced me to the Christian church. I began attending with him and was gradually being drawn back to God. The Sunday services seemed much more personal and applicable than what I was accustomed to when growing up. The Singles Ministry pastor married us, and we started attending a non-denominational church in Wellington near our home. I was determined to be solid in my faith by the time we had children, and they would begin asking questions about our beliefs.

During the first service we attended at our new church, the pastor talked about giving to those in need. Bob was planning to purchase a new car, so after service he introduced himself to the pastor and offered to donate his older car to the church. The pastor was delighted, contacted another church member who sold used cars, and traded Bob's car for two cars for single women with children in our church family. Bob was very generous and helped many families in need. He also raised funds for numerous children's organizations in Palm Beach County.

We invited the pastor to our home, and he patiently answered the many challenging questions I had about faith. I think I knew on some level that there was a void from my childhood that not even marriage and children could fill. That void would grow even larger over the next five years - a void that only God would be able to fill.

We were approached by a young man with a strong voice every week after service and invited to a small group Bible study at his home. Neither of us knew what small group Bible studies were, but we thought it would be a wonderful opportunity to meet other young couples.

The small group grew too large, and so we birthed into another group. We moved part of our small group to our home and grew larger with more young couples. That group became my family and my lifeline over the next three decades. Several of the women are still my closest friends to this day. We are born into a family, and often, God provides us with another family that walks with us through the valleys and to the mountaintops.

Couch to Couch: Gratitude is the practice of recognizing and being thankful for the blessings in your life. It involves shifting your focus away from what you lack or what is going wrong in your life, and instead, bringing to mind the positive aspects of your life, no matter how small. Even the most difficult challenges can be reframed as blessings - opportunities for learning, growth, and new beginnings.

Practical Application: Challenge yourself to start a new habit of gratitude. Here are some daily suggestions:

- ❖ **Morning Gratitude Journaling:** Start your day by writing down three things you're grateful for. You may even want to purchase a Gratitude Journal.
- ❖ **Gratitude Prayer & Meditation:** Spend a few minutes each day meditating on the things you're thankful for. Focus on your breath and let your mind bring forward moments of gratitude. Express your gratitude in prayer.
- ❖ **Gratitude Jar or Box:** Keep a jar or box where you drop a note of something you're grateful for each day. Over time, you'll have a visual reminder of all the positive things in your life.
- ❖ **Gratitude List Challenge:** As soon as you wake up, before getting out of bed, start a mental or written list of the things you are grateful for and may take for granted-waking up, your home, vision, ability to walk, food, and running water. Challenge yourself to list 100 items that you can be grateful for on a daily basis.
- ❖ **Express Appreciation to Others:** Make it a habit to tell someone you appreciate them daily. Whether it's a text, a phone call, or in person, expressing gratitude strengthens relationships.

"Mommy, I Went To Heaven"

On small group nights, a babysitter would stay with our kids in their playroom and then put them to bed. When my son was about two years old, he woke up one morning and stated, "Mommy, I went to Heaven and sat on Jesus' lap. He touched my ow (cut under his knee) and made it better."

I was still very new in my faith and quite confused at that time. I remember instantaneously wondering if he had died during the night and if he had actually visited Heaven. I considered the possibility that it was a dream. The one thing I knew for sure was that he had not made this up.

He then walked into the bathroom and picked up a small cup of Fruit Loops from the night before. I decided to question him for two distinct reasons. First, I wanted to check the validity of what he had just told me. Second, if he really had a glimpse of Heaven and Jesus, I wanted to know more.

My first question was, "What did Heaven look like?" Without hesitation, he responded, "Bright, Mommy, very bright." He then added, "Lots of colors like my Fruit Loops." He pointed to the cup of Fruit Loops that he was holding.

My next question was, "What did Jesus look like?" He looked directly at me and responded, "White, Mommy, all white." As he described the white light, he also motioned with his little hands, showing me that the light engulfed Jesus. And that was the end of our conversation. I had many more questions, but he was finished and off to play.

It is difficult to put into words the gamut of emotions I was feeling at that moment. I was teetering between amazement, fear, excitement, confusion, and disbelief. I had not taught my son about Heaven, because I knew little myself at that time. I had neither read nor studied the Book of Revelation and was even new to reading the Bible. I knew that he had not learned about Heaven in Sunday school since he was only in the one- and two-year-old nursery. The other baffling fact was that the scab on his cut where he told me Jesus touched was gone.

I soon came to learn that my son's descriptions of Heaven and Jesus were Biblically correct. I may never fully understand what occurred that night, but I believe my son had a glimpse of Heaven that God intended for me to know about.

Three years later, when my daughter was three years old, I found myself separated and in the midst of a divorce. Once again, God showed me how real and present he is in our lives. I was in the kitchen, and my daughter was playing with her toys and listening to the Disney Princesses soundtrack.

Snow White sings a song titled, "Someday My Prince Will Come." In the Bible, 1 Thessalonians 4:17 states, "Then we who are alive, who are left, will be caught up together with them in the clouds to meet the Lord in the air, and so we will always be with the Lord." Then John 14:2-3 states, "In my Father's house are many rooms. If it were not so, would I have told you that I go to prepare a place for you? And if I go and prepare a place for you, I will come again and take you to myself, that where I am you may be also."

I found this Disney princess song so comforting, and it brought to mind these verses that hugged my heart. That night I slept very peacefully and heard a song in my dream. I woke up and immediately wrote these words down. I am not musically gifted in any way and had never written lyrics to a song. These are the lyrics I penned in about 20 minutes:

> She lies alone
> Knowing no one's coming home
> But her Jesus waits for her
> And she falls asleep resting in His arms
> She wakes at three
> The night seems so long
> The night seems so dark
> Yet she recalls her dream
> And the beautiful song,
> "There's a righteous man
> He has planned for her."

Will He bring her prodigal husband home
Will she always be alone
Or will He make a way
Where she can see no way
And she cries
And she prays
That the Lord will bring
Her righteous man

Her precious three-year-old little girl
Sleeps all by herself
In her big girl bed
And she wonders how this will all affect her

She wakes at three
The night seems so long
The night seems so dark
Yet she recalls her dream
And the beautiful song,

"There's a righteous man
He has planned for her."

Will He bring her prodigal daddy home
Will they always be alone
Or will He make a way
Where she sees no way

And she cries
And she prays
That the Lord will bring
Her little girl a righteous man

She knows His promises
And she teaches her little girl about Jesus
And they cry
And they pray
Knowing someday
That He will come
And take them home
And they will never be alone

Dodging Bullets

During our engagement and early marriage, I would assist at Bob's office. The Securities and Exchange Commission (SEC), an agency of the US federal government, states as its primary purpose "to enforce the law against market manipulation," as well as to enforce securities laws, take action against wrongdoers, and protect investors. The SEC came to his office for an audit, which he was initially anxious about, but he assured me that audits were customary and there was no need for concern. He passed the audit, and he proceeded to discredit the expertise of the auditors and the SEC as a whole. They would return over the next few years, but they were never able to find any wrongful practices.

The last audit that I was informed about was around New Year's Eve in 1996 during my second pregnancy. Bob called me from his office and sounded alarmed when he informed me that, "Our house of cards could come crashing down."

"What did that even mean?" I remember feeling confused, panicked, and infuriated all at the same time. He was neither disclosing the reason for these investigations nor

planning for the protection of his pregnant wife and toddler son. Although he was again able to dodge a bullet, this investigation and its potential fallout triggered my Mama Bear instincts—claws out and determined to protect my Baby Bears at any cost.

Speaking of dodging bullets, there was an evening when Bob came home from the office late in the evening, and our children were already asleep. He walked in with several shopping bags and nonchalantly mentioned that "something happened" earlier that day.

Bob owned and wore a $25,000 Rolex diamond watch on a daily basis. I asked him not to flaunt it in public to avoid becoming a target. There was a comic book and collector's store located close to his office. He drove to the store with his car window open and his Rolex watch arm resting on the windowsill. Apparently, someone followed him into the store and put a gun to his chest. He cocked the gun and demanded the Rolex watch. Bob gave it to him. The incident was reported, then Bob continued shopping. I would have been terrified if I were in his shoes and grateful to still be alive. I would think any husband in this scenario would immediately call their wife or rush home to be with their family.

My first reaction was to cry when he told me what had happened. I could have lost my husband, and our children could have lost their father in the blink of an eye. I then found myself getting increasingly angry that he did not heed my warning. Instead of calling me after the robbery, he continued shopping and finished his workday. Most importantly, he failed to consider that by risking his life over a watch, he would have left behind a wife and two young children.

Disclosures

There was a young woman in our church who had received an inheritance and decided to invest with Bob. She informed her husband after turning over a considerable sum of money to him. The husband researched Bob's claims in his welcome packet and bio. He was suspicious of guaranteed returns stated in the packet, as well as bio information that was not verified as true. The couple asked for their money back, and the delay in returning funds raised further suspicions.

An older neighbor who considered investing with Bob also had suspicions. His son had attended the University of Miami. The neighbor inquired about Bob attending and playing football at UM, and they had no record of either.

One evening, we went on a date while our toddlers stayed with a babysitter. I remember we went to see "Good Will Hunting" in the movie theater. When we came home, we sat in the living room, and Bob began his disclosure with, "Now that we're married and have two children, I can tell you a few things." These are words you never want to hear. My stomach dropped, and I felt an overwhelming dread of what would come next.

He admitted that he not only did not have two Master's Degrees, but he didn't even have an undergraduate degree. He was never a graduate student at the University of Miami, but claims he was a walk-on for the UM national championship football team.

There was more disclosure to follow. He explained that banks invest customer's money, so if every customer walked into a bank at the same time and attempted to withdraw their money, it wouldn't be there. He continued by explaining that banks are permitted to invest deposited money, but private stockbrokers are not permitted by law to do so. This is referred to as misappropriation of funds. He had a select group of clients that he managed unlawfully or in offshore accounts but justified these practices by claiming that they were all hiding their money from spouses, family members, or the IRS.

A few years before, I witnessed a family from our church experience unimaginable losses when the husband went to prison for insurance fraud. The wife and children lost their home, all assets were frozen, and they were left utterly devastated.

I was terrified that this would happen to us. Bob tried to convince me that I was over-reacting and that I just needed to focus on taking care of our children and our home. I was convinced that we needed to prepare for the worst-case scenario and plan accordingly.

Gaslighting

So here I was, a 33-year-old mother of an infant and toddler, feeling trapped in an irretrievably broken marriage. I was living a nightmare of deception and betrayal, plagued by fear of the unknown. Trust was severely damaged and further destroyed by Bob's female "business relationships" and after-hours "business meetings." If I ever questioned these relationships or meetings, I was labeled "jealous," "paranoid," or even "bipolar." Ironically, he dated every one of these women when we separated.

Years later, I would learn that this was a psychological tactic called gaslighting. He avoided accountability for his behaviors by manipulating me into believing I was over-reacting and crazy. In reality, I was accurately perceiving these relationships and meetings. This toxic pattern started early in our relationship and continued throughout our marriage.

I remember meeting Bob for dinner one night during my first pregnancy. He came directly from work and told me about a business meeting with a foreign government leader who brought in a briefcase filled with cash. I had an extremely negative physical reaction to this business deal he described and had to leave before my meal arrived. These strong reactions occurred throughout our marriage. Every business associate that I reacted negatively to either proved to be corrupt or ill-intentioned.

A few years later, I joined Bob and two other couples for a business dinner at an Italian restaurant in South Florida. I would find out that evening that this was a known Mafia-owned establishment. Bob was meeting with his in-house accountant and the accountant's cousin, a South Florida stockbroker. While we waited for our table, we stood in the bar area.

The men talked privately while the wives got acquainted. I was discreetly listening to the conversation of the husbands. I overheard the accountant tell Bob, "My cousin knows some boys in New York and New Jersey that are going away, and before they go, they want to put some money away for their wives and children offshore." He asked if Bob could help with this. This meant they were being indicted for criminal activity and wanted to hide their money offshore.

Shortly after this conversation, a server walked by with a tray of appetizers. The cousin took one and commented that it tasted like the gourmet food at an Italian restaurant in New York. I immediately responded that we had our engagement party there. Bob later informed me that the cousin asked my family name to be sure there was no conflict between families. Of course, I pleaded that he not get involved with these men, but he refused to listen. The in-house accountant and his cousin, as well as Bob's best friend, were all eventually arrested and indicted for white-collar crimes.

I believe God has given me a spiritual gift of discernment, which is the ability to distinguish truth from falsehood, right from wrong, and good from evil, even when not in the presence of the person or persons involved. Discernment has proved to be immensely helpful with my family of origin, my marriage, and as a therapist. It has allowed me to see through lies, deception, and false teachings.

Couch to Couch: Gaslighting is a form of emotional abuse that involves manipulating or intentionally twisting a person's perception of reality. It is a psychological tactic used to gain power and control over another person by making them doubt their own thoughts, reactions, and perceptions. Victims are often left believing that they are mistaken, crazy, or overly sensitive.

Practical Application: Dealing with gaslighting by a partner or loved one can be emotionally exhausting and distressing. Here are some primary tips to help you cope if you suspect gaslighting:

- ❖ **Educate Yourself**: Learn about gaslighting to understand the tactics used and how to counteract them.
- ❖ **Recognize the Signs**: Identify behaviors that indicate gaslighting, such as denying your experiences, minimizing your feelings, or distorting reality.
- ❖ **Document Interactions**: Keep a journal of your communications and experiences. This can help you keep track of what is happening and validate your reality.
- ❖ **Build Your Support System**: Talk to trusted friends, family members, or a support group about what you're experiencing. Their perspective can provide validation of your thoughts, reactions, and perceptions.
- ❖ **Develop a Safety Plan**: If the gaslighting escalates to emotional or physical abuse, have a safety plan in place for leaving the situation.

Separation

I was feeling very desperate and requested a weekend away alone to be still, pray, and find clarity about the tough decisions that lay ahead. I found a small hotel in Ft. Lauderdale that was on the beach. I brought my Bible, some worship music, and a journal. I genuinely wanted to be still and hear from God.

Bob was convinced that I would return and ask him for a divorce. Instead, it was clear to me that we needed to downsize our lives while Bob would work on "making things right" in his business.

The first step was to sell our 6,000 square foot house. One afternoon, as I was driving past our previous neighborhood, the thought of buying back our house in Emerald Forest very strongly came to mind. Bob reluctantly spoke with his brother's wife, who was a realtor at that time. She contacted the owners and asked if they would consider selling. They accepted the offer, and we moved back into our previous home. Our Aero Club house was completely emptied and listed for sale.

Several months later, the woman who generated Bob's counterfeit monthly statements resigned, and the computers were moved into the den in our home. Bob would have to continue generating monthly statements, or his clients would be alarmed. I insisted that the computers needed to be removed from our home. I feared that our home would be raided and searched by the authorities, which would be very traumatic for our children. He reluctantly had movers empty that room.

The tension in our home could be cut with a knife. We attended one marital therapy session. He remained defensive throughout the session, and I left extremely discouraged. The following evening, we ate dinner as a family, put the kids to bed, and then he furiously filled trash bags with his clothes and left the house. He never came back.

We separated in April 1999 with no possibility of reconciliation. Our children were only 2 and 4 years old. I have to admit that parenting infants did not come naturally to me. It was a difficult adjustment becoming a parent, and now overnight I had to adjust to being a single mom. I was emotionally overwhelmed, physically exhausted, and very fearful living alone with two toddlers.

Friends suggested listening to Christian CDs or reading Psalms during the night when I couldn't sleep. In Psalm 91:11, God commands His angels to guard over us. In 2 Chronicles

3:11-13, the wingspan of the cherubim was described as 30 feet. I remember visualizing mighty angels wing to wing around my house, protecting us. My faith grew exponentially that year out of a desperate need for protection and reassurance that I was not alone. My Creator truly became my Husband and Father to my children.

Bob returned to the Aero Club house since it had not yet been sold. Shortly afterward, I was served a lawsuit. I contacted one of the many attorneys I would retain in the next few years. A civil attorney informed me that the Aero Club house was under contract. Bob had canceled the contract by forging my signature. My attorney strongly recommended that he rescind the cancellation. When I showed up for the closing, the buyers were in one room while I was shunned and led to another. Not only was I feeling deceived and betrayed again, but I was now being punished for his wrongdoing.

To add insult to injury, Bob made it clear that if I were not there to help him reach his goals, he did not need me. I genuinely believed that my only value to Bob was in fulfilling his family man image, providing a son to pass down the family name and legacy, and the caretaking of both of our mothers. This reinforced the false self-beliefs that I held from my childhood, *"I'm worthless"* and *"I'm disposable."* Let me explain how and when these self-beliefs took root.

My Roots

I was born in Flushing, Queens, New York, in the 1960s. My father was 52 when I was born and had left his wife and three teenagers—ages 12, 14, and 18. My mother was his 29-year-old mistress and insisted he marry her despite his wife never consenting to a divorce. As the story goes, my father was very politically connected and knew a judge who "married" them. It would take 35 years to find out the truth that I was born out of wedlock. That truth profoundly changed my understanding of my father's absence in my life and my half-sibling's rejection of me.

Another story my mother told for most of my life was that she wanted a girl. If I had been a boy, she would have given me to my maternal grandmother to raise. My grandmother preferred boys and helped raise my half-brother, whom my mother birthed as a teenager.

The story continued that all the gifts at the baby shower were pink, and my mother wouldn't wake up from sedation during my birth until the obstetrician repeatedly informed her that I was a girl. One of her favorite sayings was, "A son is a son till he marries a wife. A daughter is a daughter for the rest of her life." My little girl mind came to the conclusion that my only value to my mother was as a daughter who would take care of her for the rest of her life. With the help of my own therapist, I learned that this unconscious thought process translated to the core self-belief, *"I'm worthless."*

Another core belief was rooted in several experiences as a toddler. In one instance, I rolled off my bed onto a full-length mirror that was lying on the floor. The mirror cracked, and small pieces of glass had to be removed from my back. I never understood why a full-length mirror was laid on the floor next to my toddler bed.

Another day, I consumed a bottle of children's aspirin, and my stomach had to be pumped at the hospital. A few years before my mother died, she informed me that I repeated this a second time. I was sitting in the back seat of the car and consumed another bottle of children's aspirin that was in her purse. I had no recall of this second incident, but I was deeply disturbed at her carelessness as a parent. I believe these incidents were the roots of the false self-belief that *"I'm disposable."*

I was able to see years later that although my mother's purpose for my life was to take care of her, my Heavenly Father had a far greater purpose planned for me. He valued me as His child, not just as my mother's daughter.

While God created me for His purposes, I do believe there is a very real enemy that wanted to distract me from my purpose and ultimately, end my life. I've been the target of a spiritual battle throughout my life. I know beyond a doubt that God has faithfully been my protector and kept me alive to fulfill His purpose for my life.

Couch to Couch: "Sometimes you have to leave behind what you were born into to become what God intended you to be." [From "Redeeming Love" movie] Healing allows you the freedom to become all that God intended you to be.

Practical Application: These are a few of the steps required to heal childhood emotional wounds:

- ❖ **Awareness:** Acknowledge honestly to yourself what you were born into and all of the related emotions.
- ❖ **Grief Process:** Allow yourself to grieve what was stolen from you as a child (innocence, trust, security, safety) and the emotional needs that were unmet.
- ❖ **Forgiveness:** Choose to go through the forgiveness process in order to let go of all resentment and roots of bitterness.

Core Self-Beliefs

I have very few memories of my father during my childhood and no recollection of him living with us. The one memory I do have with my father is going to Palisades Amusement Park as a young child. I can vividly remember riding the roller coaster together. When I turned 10, my father opened a local amusement park, Adventurer's Inn, which he built. Adventurer's Inn was reviewed as "the most beloved of the restaurant parks," opening in 1950 and closed by the city in 1978.

Frequent visits and birthday parties at the amusement park temporarily filled some of the void left by my father's absence in our home. Food filled the rest. It makes sense that amusement parks and food have served the same purpose in my adulthood—to temporarily fill the void of abandonment and rejection.

I was not told that I had half-siblings until I was 18 years old. Within that year, my father took my youngest half-sister, my half-brother, and me to Atlantic City to meet each other. I recall my half-sister commenting, "Why is she here?" I remember feeling very hurt and rejected.

I was invited to dinner at my oldest half-sister's home that same year. After dinner, we were talking in the kitchen, and she informed me that it was difficult for her to be around me because I reminded her of her father leaving 18 years prior. This message translated in my teenage mind to *"I'm responsible for causing emotional pain,"* and therefore, rejected simply for being born.

My father had already raised three children, and I assumed he did not plan for an infant at the age of 52. In my mind, this was the only explanation for why he was absent for most of my childhood. The false self-belief that took root was *"I'm unwanted."*

My father served in World War II as an engineer and received a Military Funeral Honors Ceremony, which included folding and presenting the United States burial flag and the playing of "Taps." His other life achievements included building beautiful homes in Jamaica Estates, NY, and constructing Adventurer's Inn Amusement Park and Desert Inn Beach Club & Night Club in College Point, NY. Sadly, his children and grandchildren don't have many personal memories of him. Personally, I want to leave a legacy of being present and impactful in the lives of my family, friends, and others.

NOW is the time to build your legacy. You are only given one lifetime. Your family and friends will remember more about how you lived and loved others than your wealth and achievements.

Couch to Couch: Children try to make sense of their world from an early age by asking questions. When adults act in senseless ways toward a child, that child may be overtly threatened or covertly silenced to not speak to anyone. The child will still try to make sense in their own mind. Often, the sense they make is that they are defective, damaged, or undesirable for some reason.

Children then wrongly conclude that they are the cause of abuse, abandonment, rejection, and other senseless adult behaviors. Core self-beliefs such as, *"I'm unwanted," "I'm not good enough," and "I don't matter"* take root. These core self-beliefs can affect thoughts, feelings, behaviors, decisions, and relationships well into adulthood.

Practical Application: Negative self-beliefs can be changed. The first and most important step in the change process is awareness. Sometimes you have to visit your past in order to understand your present:

- ❖ Start by asking yourself and close family members questions about your past.
- ❖ Bring to mind significant memories that deeply impacted or wounded you.
- ❖ Ask yourself, "What lies did I believe about myself based on how I was treated or spoken to earlier in life?"

Repetition Compulsion

When I was 18 months old, my mother and I lived in Puerto Rico with a man named Raul. He was a casino manager and lived in Condado Beach. I remember him as a tall, gentle man, and his home felt like a safe place. In my 30s, I found out from my father that my mother took me to Puerto Rico, married Raul, and wrote my father a "Dear John" letter.

In more recent years, I also found out that Raul left his wife and four children to live with my mother and me. My mother had met him years before I was born, so as an adult, I wondered if he was my biological father. It was difficult to understand why a man would leave his family to care for a woman and her toddler unless he believed he was my father.

I recall that my mother and I lived between Puerto Rico and New York for most of my toddler years. My brother, who was 13 years older than me, lived with my grandmother while attending school.

Between 3 and 5 years old, my mother, brother, and I lived in an apartment building in Flushing, NY. My brother babysat for me when my mother worked. I remember one night when my mother was violently attacked by a stranger running upstairs in our building. It would take 43 years to find out from a family friend that the man who stabbed her in the back of her head was an abusive boyfriend, George—not a stranger.

He was another man in my mother's life for many years. His real name was Vincent, but my mother and family members called him Jim. I was told his name was George so that I would not speak his name in front of my father on the rare occasions that he visited. I'm guessing George was enraged by my mother's relationship choices when I was young. I also questioned if George believed he was my father. This would explain—though not justify—his rage when my mother took me to Puerto Rico and married another man.

At age five, we moved into the house I lived in until I was 26. Raul helped my mother with the down payment. We vacationed in Puerto Rico for several years until they divorced.

George came back into our lives during my elementary school years. He was a very unsafe, critical, enraged man with the added complications of diabetes and alcoholism. He was the main contributor to another false belief that "*All men are unsafe.*"

That belief was strengthened on Thanksgiving Day 1982 when we returned home from my grandmother's holiday dinner. I could hear George provoking a fight with my mother under the influence of alcohol. The next memory is hearing my mother scream and running into the living room to find blood gushing down her face. George had punched her and broken her nose. He ran out the front door and never returned. My brother verbally threatened his life, which helped to keep him away.

Five years later, my mother received a call from a woman that George lived with. He was recovering from cancer surgery and repeatedly called out my name while waking from the anesthesia. She looked in his phone book, found our names, and called to inform us of his condition. My mother and I visited him in Mercy Hospital until he died.

I was in graduate school at that time and began my own therapy at the recommendation of two close classmates and my clinical supervisor. Unresolved trauma and loss issues were manifesting in symptoms of repressed anger, depression, anxiety, addictive behaviors, and repeated dysfunctional relationships. I knew I had to address my own issues before I could effectively help others. This marked the beginning of a lifelong healing process.

Couch to Couch: When you believe deep down inside that you're worthless, unwanted, damaged, or disposable, you tend to unknowingly put yourself in situations or relationships that perpetuate this belief. This often becomes a pattern throughout adulthood until you intentionally explore your past and identify your core self-beliefs. Only then, can you break through limiting beliefs and replace them with positive truths about yourself.

Practical Application: There is a psychological phenomenon called Repetition Compulsion, which is the unconscious process of repeating negative relationship patterns that are familiar and often rooted in childhood trauma. When you find yourself unknowingly attracted to people who share the characteristics of a parent or parental figure and, in some way, hurt you early in life.

In the beginning of a relationship, these characteristics are barely noticeable. Your brain seems to have a built-in radar system that can detect these traits. Your unconscious wish may be to master situations in which you felt powerless in order to heal wounds through familiar but new relationships. Unfortunately, by choosing familiar relationships, you may often repeat negative patterns and reopen wounds instead of healing them.

Awareness is the first step to breaking these self-destructive patterns.

My Safety Net

My brother was my safety net. He was 13 years old when I was born. Before my mother passed away, I asked her about my birth. She fondly recalled how my brother sat in a chair and held me in the hospital. When it was time to be discharged, my brother refused to hand me over to the nurse. Instead, he carried me to the car and held me in his arms throughout the entire ride home.

Our bedrooms were next to each other on the second floor of the house we lived in. I can remember waking up during the night between the ages of 5 and 7, either standing in his doorway or next to his bed until he woke up and patiently guided me back to my own bed.

Though I don't have conscious memories of missing my brother while we lived in Puerto Rico, I'm sure the separation was difficult. He was my protector and my hero until he decided to get married and move out when I was 8 years old. Both decisions made no sense to me, and I was determined to show my disapproval in every wedding picture taken. I made spiteful faces and refused to smile for even one picture. Unfortunately, that did not change either of his decisions.

The most significant and devastating loss in my life has been the death of my brother in 2006. He was diagnosed with pancreatic cancer on my mother's 70th birthday and died five months later. I realized that he died when my daughter was 8 years old. As I watched my daughter mourn the loss of her favorite uncle - at the same age that I grieved the loss of my big brother when he married - my own grief was doubled.

Couch to Couch: In my decades of counseling individuals, couples, and families, I have seen a familial pattern repeat over and over again. Parents often experience heightened emotions and psychological or physical symptoms when children are at the same age that they experienced trauma or significant losses during their own childhood.

I've even observed couples experiencing emotions that they had stored away at the age of their children, thereby reliving family dynamics from their own upbringing. Their false core beliefs are often unknowingly triggered by each other as well. I have found women often feel unloved and believe "*I don't matter*," while men often feel disrespected and believe "*I'm not good enough*," just like when they were children.

Practical Application: I use a therapy tool called a genogram to diagram familial relationships and patterns. Particularly when clients present with unexplained symptoms, I note the ages of their children and ask what was happening in their lives at that age. They almost always begin to recall a traumatic event or significant loss, and then ask how I knew. I explain that children are like little mirrors of them. When parents look at their child, they unconsciously see themself at the same age.

Surrogate Spouse

Once my brother moved out, my mother decided to rent out the upstairs floor to supplement her income, and I shared her bed until I was 14 years old. For six years, I served as her surrogate spouse. The boundary between where she ended and I began was unclear. Her fears became my own when she would wake me up during the night frightened by noises.

It wasn't until I started sleeping over at friends' houses at age 14 that I realized kids had their own bedrooms and their own beds. I demanded my own space too. The sunroom, which was built on, became my bedroom. Although she allowed for this physical boundary, the emotional boundaries were never respected.

When I went to college, I yearned to experience dorm life as a door to independence. However, this was strongly discouraged, and instead, I attended a local university for my undergraduate degree.

Graduate school took me further from home. I planned to rent a basement apartment from my classmate. I used my older car as an excuse to convince my mother that the daily commute would be too much. In a very loving and generous act, she purchased a new car for me. I was deeply grateful for the car and lived at home for the next four years.

My first experience with therapy was during graduate school. I was considering moving to Florida after graduation but was convinced that my mother would develop cancer and die. Her continual reminders that my leaving would "kill her" instilled that fear in me. I already harbored the belief that "*I'm responsible for causing emotional pain.*" Now, another false belief took root: "*I'm responsible for people's lives.*"

This belief was further reinforced years later when I visited my mother's sister in New York. I had planned a surprise 70th birthday party for my mother at my aunt's home. On the morning of the party, my aunt had a heart attack and was hospitalized. It was implied that the stress of our visit and the birthday celebration triggered the heart attack. The false belief that "*I'm responsible for people's lives*" was further reinforced.

Therapy helped me identify and break through these false beliefs. I courageously moved to Florida in 1990. My mother did not develop cancer and die. She did, however, start taking antidepressants to help her cope.

Within three years of my relocation, my mother purchased a condo in Florida. She retired and moved into the condo two years later. She was a snowbird during the summer months, staying in her house in New York.

Breaking out of the parentified child role was incredibly difficult. My mother continued to depend on me to meet her emotional needs and be her caretaker. She never remarried. When I married and had my children, I was able to set limited boundaries with her. Unfortunately, boundaries were often disregarded and misperceived as rejection, so I walked a tightrope for many years.

Couch to Couch: Parentifying a child occurs when a parent allows the child to stand in for a spouse after divorce or death and depends on the child to meet their emotional needs. The role of surrogate spouse places a heavy burden on the child, leaving them feeling hopeless and helpless, as they lack the coping skills or life experience to deal with their parent's problems and emotions.

Practical Application: Relinquishing the role of surrogate spouse to a parent can be challenging but is essential for fostering healthy relationships and emotional well-being. Here are several steps to help navigate this process:

- ❖ Recognize and admit to yourself that you have been acting as a surrogate spouse. Reflect on how this role has affected your life and relationships.
- ❖ Journal your experiences and feelings about this role to gain clarity.
- ❖ Plan a calm, open and honest conversation with your parent about the need to redefine your relationship. Express your feelings and the importance of establishing a healthier dynamic.
- ❖ Write down the boundaries you need, such as limiting emotional support to appropriate levels or ensuring you have personal time.
- ❖ Establish and communicate specific boundaries that will help you maintain a healthier relationship. Be firm and consistent in enforcing these boundaries.
- ❖ Focus on developing your personal interests, hobbies, and social connections outside of your role with your parent. This will create a sense of independence and fulfillment.

My Heavenly Father

Now that I've explained the childhood roots of my negative self-beliefs, I will continue with the false narrative that I've been replaying in my mind for the past 20 years. Back to my marriage.

Bob moved out of our home in April 1999. I attended a Christian retreat in Georgia called Healing for the Nations several months later. One powerful exercise we were guided through was listing the character traits of God the Father and Jesus His Son. The challenge was to list the traits we genuinely attributed to each, not just what we were taught in Sunday school growing up. I was surprised to learn that I attributed vastly contrasting character traits to God and Jesus. In my mind, God was an old man figure who resided in Heaven, was emotionally detached, even uninterested in my life, and was a punitive, punishing Father. I gave Him all the same traits as my earthly, biological father.

In contrast, I described Jesus as emotionally available, nurturing, comforting, and protective, which were the same traits as my brother. I remember him as being very loving and protective my entire childhood.

A Christian author stated, "We have to wipe the face of our father off the face of God." I began to view God's character more accurately once I forgave my father and desired to reconcile our relationship.

I visited my father in NY several months after the retreat. I had felt led to fast for 21 days as Daniel fasted in the Bible. I brought my father a large-print Bible since he was 87 years old at that time. He truthfully answered every question I asked him about the circumstances around my birth, his relationship with my mother, and his lack of involvement in my life. This is when he explained that his wife never consented to a divorce. He further explained that my mother was angry that he wouldn't live with us, and as an act of vengeance, kept me from him. He assured me that he was my biological father, which I had questioned for many years.

Over the next six months, my father read the entire Bible cover to cover. On the following Father's Day, I called him, and we prayed together over the phone. My father had brain surgery after two falls in his apartment later that year. After the surgery, I was standing at his bedside with my half-sister. He told us that he was not afraid to die since he knew he would be with Jesus in Heaven. He had an incredible sense of peace despite having brain surgery at 88 years old.

I confided in one of the leaders at this retreat that my husband was involved in illegal business activities. I was counseled to speak with an attorney to find out if I would be protected in the event that he was arrested. I already had the business card of a Christian family law attorney and scheduled an appointment when I returned from the retreat.

I began to explain my circumstances to the attorney. There happened to be a criminal attorney in the upstairs office in the same building. She contacted the criminal attorney, and I met with her right after my session. I again explained my circumstances. She excused herself and contacted another criminal attorney. She returned and informed me that this attorney had an opening and wanted me to come right over to his office. I knew that it was difficult to schedule appointments with attorneys, so I attributed this to God opening the door for me that same day.

I found myself in the office of a high-profile criminal attorney. After a brief conversation, he informed me that he could not represent me due to a conflict of interest. One of the attorneys in his practice was from my church and was also a client of Bob's. That attorney was able to remove his money from Bob's firm. The attorney informed me that I would not have immunity if Bob were arrested since I knew of his illegal activity and reaped financial gain as a stay-at-home mom.

In addition, it is common for wives and adult children to be named officers in a corporation. I was unknowingly named the Vice President of his corporation and put on the payroll. At that moment, I knew that Bob was not protecting me or his children. I would have to take every step possible to keep us safe.

During our separation, I voiced my concerns about our kids being kidnapped for ransom or revenge. I was made to believe I was overreacting and paranoid. Not until a decade later did he admit to hiring security guards to follow me and our children on outings. As I had discerned, the threats were real.

Bob also admitted that the criminal attorney was his friend and had contacted him 15 minutes after I left the office. The attorney then informed a partner in his firm who represented his organized crime clientele. They allegedly planned to "take care of the wife" so that I would not disclose any information to the authorities.

Many years later, Bob informed me that my father had introduced him to the organized crime clientele in New York during our engagement. I was devastated to learn that my own father introduced Bob to the men who would eventually threaten my life. The depth of betrayal that I felt toward my father and ex-husband was beyond words.

I had to work through the tsunami of emotions I experienced related to their betrayal. It has taken many years to really grieve these losses and choose forgiveness.

My Heavenly Father has healed me from the wounds incurred by my earthly father and husband. Where my earthly parents and husband were careless with my life, my Heavenly Father has valued and preserved my life. There is no other explanation in my mind for how I am still alive today and have been protected from known and unknown threats throughout my life.

Queen Esther

I was constantly plagued with the question, "*What do I do with what I know?*" This was an extremely complicated matter because Bob was still my husband and the father of our children. While I had been downsizing our lives, he was extravagantly spending.

To further complicate matters, Bob was managing life savings for family, friends, and church members. The more clients he took on, the more lives that would be devastated if he were arrested.

A phrase that went through my mind daily was, "*Evil prevails when good men do nothing.*" I scheduled meetings with church leaders and members to seek wise counsel but was not encouraged to take action. Only one small group member earnestly prayed with me and counseled me to, "Do the right thing."

During this time, I learned a lot of Bible stories through a computer animated video series called Veggie Tales that I enjoyed watching with my kids. The video "Esther, The Girl

Who Became Queen" was newly released. The subtitle was "A Lesson In Courage" which conveyed the message, *"You never need to be afraid to do what is right."*

The Book of Esther is found in the Old Testament and tells the story of a young Jewish girl who becomes Queen. She risks her life by going uninvited to her husband, King Xerxes, which was punishable by death, to inform him that his right-hand man, Haman, is plotting to harm her cousin Mordecai and the Jewish people. In the Bible, Mordecai tells Esther, "For if you keep silent at this time, . . . you and your father's house will perish. And who knows whether you have not come to the kingdom for such a time as this?" (Esther 4:14) In the end, Esther saves the lives of her people.

After watching that video, I felt a nudge to read the Book of Esther in the Bible. I put the kids to bed and sat on the back patio. When I came to the verse above, I knew God was giving me clear direction to do the right thing by not remaining silent. I also learned that although we are told to seek wise counsel in the Bible, ultimately, we need to listen to God's counsel. I just needed to be still long enough to hear His direction, which He provided to me step-by-step.

A short time after reading the Book of Esther, I prayed for God's direction regarding the next step I should take. Right before a meeting with a member of our small group, I remember very specifically asking God to show me a church member with a friend in the FBI. When the small group member arrived, his first words were that he spoke to an attorney who attended our church and had a friend in the FBI. Shortly afterward, the FBI agent requested a meeting with me.

It was clear to me that not only does God hear and answer our prayers, but He will also show us how to pray. The only explanation I have for so specifically asking for a church member with a friend in the FBI is that God's Holy Spirit guided my words. This was yet another confirmation of how real and personal God is when we wholeheartedly seek Him.

FBI Meeting

In September 2000, the attorney from our church represented me, and we attended the meeting requested by the FBI agent. That morning, I went through our daily routine at home, then prepared lunch for my kids and my mother, who would be staying with them. This was an extremely distressing and surreal day.

It was hard to wrap my mind around my incredulous circumstances. I was living a nightmare that I couldn't wake up from. It took every ounce of my emotional and physical energy to get through each day as a single mom and informant to the FBI. I spiraled down into depression, fear, and overwhelming worry for the future. Every day was a challenge as I learned to trust God completely.

My attorney met me at the FBI building. I remember feeling very anxious about either Bob or someone he knows seeing me enter that building. When we exited the elevator, the wall straight ahead had the FBI logo signage. If anyone had entered the elevator with us, they would definitely know where we were going.

We went through a security check, then met with an FBI agent and the United States Attorney. Their first question for me was, "Why was I there and willing to meet with them?" I explained that it was the right thing to do and that I did not want more people's lives devastated by my remaining silent. Most importantly, I felt an immense sense of responsibility for taking every measure possible to protect our 3- and 5-year-old children.

They asked me several specific questions about Bob, then informed me that he had already been under investigation and that I had provided the "missing pieces of the puzzle." I was asked to meet with the United States Attorney at his office about a week later.

More than a year passed after those meetings. The FBI continued their investigation and gathered more evidence. Our divorce was finalized several months after the meetings. It was a really difficult year trying to continue with the daily routine of a single mom while preparing for the inevitable disruption in all of our lives.

Helping Children Grieve

The year 2001 brought several difficult and traumatic events. Early that year, I found a pea-size lump in my breast and had it surgically removed. On the day of the surgery, I walked outside and a skywriter had just finished creating the message, "Jesus loves you." Those were very comforting words to see across the sky.

My maternal grandmother was 89 years old and living with my mother. She had been diagnosed with Alzheimer's Disease about seven years before and had full-time caretakers. Whenever there was a medical emergency, my mother would call the paramedics, and then call me; I would follow the ambulance to the hospital.

My grandmother died in August 2001 when my children were 4 and 6 years old. The last time my children were with their great-grandmother was when we visited her in the hospital. I reassured them that the hospital did not cause her death so that they would not be fearful if I were ever hospitalized.

This was the first death of a close family member, so I purchased children's books that talked about death and loss and read to them. I encouraged my children to ask questions and put their feelings into words. I expressed my sadness and allowed them to see me cry. I explained to them that just as their favorite toys stop working and can't be fixed, our bodies stop working and can't be fixed when we're old or extremely sick.

I reminded my son of the vision he had of Heaven as a toddler, and that one day we would all be reunited. I can only imagine the indescribable joy we will experience when that day comes.

Couch to Couch: In my early years as a therapist, I pursued specialized bereavement training. I was working at a community counseling center where several young clients had lost a parent, so I developed a grief and loss group. The children who participated had many questions about death that they feared asking the surviving parent. These children were great teachers of their unique grief process.

Young children have magical thinking and may believe they have caused a death or can stop or reverse a death. It's also difficult for young children to grasp the finality of death. A very poignant example was when one little girl in this group asked why she wasn't able to open her father's eyes at his viewing. She believed that opening his eyes would have brought him back to life.

After speaking with a funeral director, I was able to honestly answer her question. I then gently and compassionately explained that his body had stopped working and that even if she opened his eyes, he would not have come back to life. A very heavy burden was lifted off her shoulders by allowing her to ask questions and verbalize her feelings in a safe place.

Practical Application:

- ❖ Talking openly about sad feelings and even crying in front of children gives them permission to express themselves.
- ❖ Parental expression of grief is **not** helpful if parents avoid talking openly about death and loss with their children.
- ❖ Parents need to reach out to other adults or a counselor to support them through the grieving process and to prevent children from becoming their source of comfort.
- ❖ Reading children's books on the subject of grief and loss gives children permission to ask questions and put their feelings into words.

Ponzi Scheme

On October 31, 2001, I was preparing for a neighborhood event in our community clubhouse when I received a call from a close friend inquiring why the FBI was searching Bob's home. That night, I watched the local news and had my questions answered in the cover story. He was being investigated for a Ponzi scheme, and his computers and files were being confiscated by the authorities. He had not yet been arrested.

One week later, I was at Chuck E. Cheese's with my children for Wednesday night visitation with their father. I had a strange foreboding as I entered the building and immediately noticed a brawny man wearing an earpiece. I would later find out that he was an FBI agent and that the building was surrounded by other agents. They had planned to take Bob into custody after I left with the kids. The only problem was that he never showed up.

The following day, he was arrested at his home and indicted for a "$33 Million Ponzi Scheme." Ten months later, he was sentenced to 25 years in federal prison. This was the cover story on the local news and the front-page story of the

Palm Beach Post for several weeks. The story was also covered nationally.

The story was even more sensationalized by the timing of his arrest—the day before his charitable foundation's celebrity event at the Mar-a-Lago Club and the Trump International Golf Club. The entire weekend event was canceled, resulting in a devastating monetary loss for the non-profit organizations, the vendors, his clients, and all who had paid a significant amount to participate in the weekend events. He probably would have been arrested even earlier, but the World Trade Center towers were attacked on September 11th, which delayed the FBI.

I received several phone calls from reporters, but I explained that we had been separated and divorced for two years, so I was quite removed from his business world. I was mentioned in several newspaper articles and a local magazine. One newspaper article stated that my "whereabouts were unknown." I remember walking into my son's kindergarten classroom and his teacher stating, "I know where you are!" in reference to the article. We both had a much-needed laugh.

One afternoon, I was sitting on a swing chair in front of my house reading a book to my kids. We went inside for a few minutes, and the doorbell rang. It was a reporter from People magazine. I declined an interview and was grateful that my kids were inside the house.

It was a very real concern that clients, particularly those involved in organized crime, would take revenge on my children since Bob was in prison, and they would no longer have access to their funds. Friends of ours lived in the same community where Bob lived when he was arrested. The wife was walking around the neighborhood shortly after his arrest and saw a rag doll at his front door with a knife in its chest and fake blood. It was a very disturbing sight and message.

I had considered moving out of state with my children to protect them from vengeful clients. My closest friends were concerned for my life as well. Once again, I had to put all of my trust in God to protect my children and me. He has faithfully kept us safe for the past 25 years.

Prison

Our grieving process really began two years earlier when my children experienced the loss of their father living with us. They enjoyed spending time with their dad and his mother on weekends and mid-week at fun places, but they really didn't understand all the changes happening in their little world.

It was exceedingly difficult explaining separation and divorce to a 2- and 4-year-old. Fortunately, I was able to find children's books on this subject. The local bookstore carried a book about dinosaurs divorcing and another book where Mr. Rogers talks about divorce. Children can relate to the characters in books, so reading to them and then talking with them was helpful.

I compare this period of separation and divorce to a loved one receiving a terminal diagnosis. Emotions ranged from shock and disbelief that this was happening to feeling powerless, fearful, and a sense of dread for the unknown future. The actual finalizing of the divorce symbolized the death of a marriage—grieving the past, present, and future dreams and losses.

My children's grief was further compounded when their father went to prison. They were too young to understand what had happened to him and where he was. They not only lost daily contact with him, but all of their personal belongings, including toys from his home, were removed and auctioned.

Many other complications arose following their father's arrest. Eventually, they asked where he was. I refused to tell them that their father was on a business trip as he requested. Due to their concrete thinking, if I ever traveled for work, they might have feared I wouldn't return. I explained that their father broke grown-up rules called laws and had to go to an adult time-out and stay there.

When they asked why he went there, I would not tell them it was a consequence of speeding as he requested. Their concrete thinking could trigger the fear that if I were ever stopped for a traffic violation, I would be taken away. In fact, this exact scenario occurred a few months later.

I was driving with my kids in the backseat when a police officer pulled me over. I had not stopped long enough at a stop sign. I immediately looked in the rearview mirror and saw their terrified little faces. As I anticipated, they were fearful that I would go away just like their father. The officer gave me a warning, and I reassured them that I was not going anywhere.

My next thought was to call my son's hockey coach, who was also a police officer. We went to his home, and he further reassured them that I would not be arrested and taken away for a driving violation. I knew they needed to hear that directly from a law enforcement officer.

In February 2002, I drove with my mother-in-law to Miami for the kids to visit their father. He had to complete a visitors list ahead of time and assured me that I was on the list to escort the kids inside for their visit. The drive took an hour, then we had to sign in and wait another hour. I was called to the registration window and informed that I was not on the list. My mother-in-law quickly volunteered to take the kids inside since she was an approved visitor.

I remember watching my 4- and 6-year-olds go through security, down a long hallway, and through a locked door. I waved to them through the glass, walked outside, and sobbed. Indescribable fear and helplessness overcame me as I watched my two preschoolers go through security to visit their father without me there to comfort and protect them. I couldn't imagine what they would witness and experience during that visit. I was incredibly grateful when they came out and were excited that they had soda and ice cream with their dad and nana. I knew that God heard my prayer and was with them during their visit.

Children of parents in prison are often referred to as "silent victims." They suffer the consequences of the parent's incarceration and are often overlooked and stigmatized by society.

Finding children's books that talk about this subject has been challenging. I was therefore inspired to write the children's book, "Hope: When Someone You Love Goes To Jail," to validate these children's feelings and convey that they are not alone.

Couch to Couch: I believe it is important to be truthful with children and provide them with age-appropriate information. Children can understand the concept of "time-out for grown-ups" when they are too young to comprehend the legal system and incarceration. Describing the criminal acts committed is too burdensome for children. I gave my kids a simple explanation that their father's job was to take care of other people's money and that he broke rules.

In addition to being truthful, it is equally important to be respectful of the other parent. In my years as a family therapist, as well as with my own children, I have learned that children understand they are a part of both parents. If either parent is berated, devalued, or harshly judged in front of children, they will believe they possess the same negative character traits or patterns of behavior as that parent.

Compounded Trauma

After visiting the Miami Correctional Facility, I was infuriated with my ex-husband for lying about putting me on the visitor's list. I did not trust him and his mother alone with our children. When he was first arrested, his mother and her long-term boyfriend hid Bob's highly valuable comic books and refused to turn them over to the authorities. The authorities threatened to arrest his mother, and the story was in the local news.

I lost trust in my mother-in-law and her boyfriend when Bob and I were separated and divorcing. Bob called me one day and left a voicemail asking if I suspected that his mother's boyfriend was ever inappropriate with our children. This was a very disturbing message to receive, particularly since I never fully trusted her boyfriend. Bob explained that the boyfriend was involved in an extortion case where he had to pay $1,000 to avoid explicit photos of him being posted on the internet.

The next morning, I received a call from the Sheriff's Office Special Victims Unit. The officer asked if I was aware that the boyfriend was involved in an extortion case with a prostitution ring. He also wanted to ensure that my children had not been molested by him.

I had talked to my children prior to this incident and explained to them that their bodies are private and that no one is allowed to touch them. I again talked with my children and felt assured that he had never been inappropriate with them. I then went to the Sheriff's Office and obtained a copy of the police report.

I can remember feeling nauseated and disgusted when I read the report. The boyfriend had hired an underage female prostitute who turned out to be a male transvestite, so he refused to pay for services. He met them in the bank parking lot outside the 55+ community where they lived. When I confronted my mother-in-law, she admitted that "he liked young girls." She had no intention of ending her relationship with him, so I forbade them from spending time with my children when he was around.

I allowed the kids to spend the night at Christmas time in 2001 after their father was arrested. My mother-in-law allowed her boyfriend to be there and tried to keep it from me. My kids had already been through the trauma of marital separation, divorce, and incarceration, and I would not tolerate them being around this man with a sexually perverted history. I chose to sever ties with my mother-in-law and her boyfriend to protect my young children. She filed a lawsuit against me for Grandparent Rights. I had to hire an attorney, but she was not awarded visitation rights.

My mother lived in the same community as my mother-in-law and her boyfriend at that time. My mother disclosed the extortion case to friends while at her pool and implied that he was a pedophile. Word got back to my mother-in-law, and they filed a Defamation of Character lawsuit against my mother. I again had to hire an attorney to represent my mother.

In the end, she had to pay them $8,000 and write a letter of apology. They took that letter, photocopied it, and hung it on the message board in each building with my mother's name and phone number, as well as the words, "Do you know your neighbor?" Of course, they never admitted to it, but years later, when I took my kids to visit their grandmother in Georgia, I found those photocopies. I also found a letter from Bob to his mother directing her to contact an attorney and file the Defamation of Character lawsuit. He denied knowing anything about the lawsuit.

My mother-in-law had moved to Georgia with her boyfriend, and they eventually married. In 2013, he died suddenly of a heart attack. She was in poor health and not able to stand or walk on her own. His 30-year-old grandson drove to Georgia, emptied their rental home, drove all of their belongings and vehicles to Florida, and took my mother-in-law to his mobile home. She had to be hospitalized shortly after arriving in Florida. He was not able to care for her, and my ex-husband was expecting my children, then 15 and 17 years old, to take over her care, obtain Medicaid, and find a facility for her to reside in. My children were not capable of, nor should they have been expected to take over her care.

I stepped in and assisted with setting up a trust for her deceased husband's life insurance policy, initiating the Medicaid process, and transferring her to a skilled nursing facility. My son was away at college, so my daughter and I would visit regularly. We bought her new clothes and shoes, and we took her laundry home each week. Her belongings were stored in my garage.

We brought her to my home for the holidays. I took over her care for a year. I then contacted her sister and brother in Pennsylvania and requested they bring her up north and take over caring for her. She was my ex-mother-in-law. I needed to focus on helping my own mother.

Couch to Couch: If you have aging parents or terminally ill family members, it is critically important to consult with an estate planning attorney or elder law attorney to protect personal assets in the event that a skilled nursing facility or home health care (neither covered by Medicare) is required.

Medicaid will cover skilled nursing facilities (SNF) and home health care, but you may not have more than $2,000 in personal assets, and there is a five-year look-back period (once you move assets into a trust, you are not eligible for Medicaid for five years).

In addition to protecting assets, an attorney will assist with a Last Will & Testament, Living Will, Health Care Surrogate (authority to make medical decisions if your loved one is incapacitated), and Power of Attorney (authority to make non-medical decisions). I also strongly suggest being a co-signer on bank accounts.

For elderly parents, there is an option to pre-pay funeral and burial arrangements. When a loved one passes, it is often a very emotional time, making it extremely difficult to plan the funeral and burial.

Remarriage

In December 2001, I was introduced to a single man, Harry, by a close friend. I had been separated from Bob since May 1999, and our divorce was finalized in December 2000. Although I wanted to be married again and provide a family unit for my children, I was very guarded and not interested in the dating scene.

Harry was a personal trainer at the gym where my friend's husband worked out, and they got to know each other over several months. My friend asked if I would be interested in meeting him. He was invited to a holiday party with our friend group for our first meeting.

After the party, he asked me out on a date. We went to a restaurant and then walked around for several hours. I disclosed to him the circumstances surrounding my divorce and my ex-husband's arrest. He asked me how I was able to get through these difficult circumstances, at which point I shared my faith and dependence on God.

In hindsight, there were a few red flags on that date. My faith had grown strong during the previous five years, and I knew my future husband would have to share my beliefs. Although that was not the case with Harry, he was interested to know more and would engage in deep discussions about faith.

Over time, we continued dating and committed to a long-term relationship. He began attending church and small group Bible study with me, and when my daughter wanted to be water baptized, he joined her. Sadly, several years into the marriage, he stopped attending our small group and church and rejected my beliefs.

Another concern for me on our first date was that I no longer drank alcohol, which I told him when the server was taking our order. I expected that he would then also not order a drink since he didn't yet know my reason for not drinking. There was always the possibility that I was sober and in recovery, but he ordered a drink anyway.

He had been married and divorced twice before. He disclosed that he was unfaithful in his second marriage. While we were dating and married, his lack of boundaries with women was concerning. I did not have any close male friends, only female friends. He almost exclusively had female friends and co-workers with whom he would spend time and talk on the phone.

Harry never fathered biological children, which I initially thought would be beneficial if we were to marry. Remarriage has challenges of its own without the additional challenge of blending families. The combination of no experience parenting young children, as well as step-parenting children with trauma histories, was a serious stressor throughout our marriage.

Couch to Couch: In my years as a therapist, I have witnessed that friendships of the opposite sex in a marriage very often cause serious problems. Either one or both parties inevitably develop romantic or sexual feelings, and at the very least, these friendships lead to the other spouse feeling jealous and betrayed. Even if they never have a sexual affair, the connection can feel like an emotional affair, especially to women. Wives want to know that they have an exclusive "window into their husband's heart."

Many women experience similar feelings of jealousy and betrayal when husbands watch pornography or go to strip clubs. Wives often compare themselves to these women and feel unattractive and undesirable to their husbands.

Couch to Couch: Step-families and step-parenting bring many unique and challenging dynamics into a marriage. As a therapist, I've sought specific training on this subject to better educate and counsel my clients. Ron Deal is an author, therapist, and blended family specialist. His books on step-families and step-parenting are excellent resources.

Legal Fallout

Bob remained in the Miami Federal Detention Center until his sentencing hearings in September 2002. Harry and I got engaged in May 2002 and attended all of the sentencing hearings. I needed closure and wanted to understand the extent of the criminal activity he was being indicted for. I wasn't prepared to hear the testimonies of his victims, several of whom I had met and who were truly kind to me and my children when they were young.

Numerous victims were elderly and lost their entire life savings. One victim took his own life. Another had a fatal heart attack. A couple lost funds they had saved to care for their disabled adult son when they passed. Many lives were devastated.

The final sentencing hearing was on September 14, 2002, the day before our wedding. We still attended the hearing, and Bob was sentenced to 25 years in federal prison. Even my attorney was surprised at the length of the sentence. The victims finally believed justice was served.

We had our wedding the next day. My friends had a beautiful home on the lake in the same community where my ex-husband had lived when he was arrested. They kindly hosted our backyard lakefront wedding.

Our honeymoon was in the Keys on Little Palm Island. It was a much-needed respite from the stressors we left behind. Little did I know that the sentencing would be the impetus for yet another round of legal issues. We returned from our honeymoon to several lawsuits.

One lawsuit was filed by Bob's clients against me for $500,000. He was a pilot who worked with our friends that lived in the Aero Club. I believe that the husband encouraged this pilot to sue me for this large amount of money. I again hired an attorney but did not have the funds to pay this client and was already under litigation with the bankruptcy attorneys.

The other lawsuit was filed by the bankruptcy attorneys against me for $1,500,000 and against my mother since Bob managed her money and paid her monthly bills from his business account. I had to hire representation for both myself and my mother.

Prior to sentencing, there were auctions held for Bob's automobiles, furniture, collectibles, watches, and even the children's toys that were at his house. The bankruptcy attorneys used the money from the auctions to compensate the victims for their losses and to pay legal fees. Unfortunately, only a fraction of the losses were compensated for, so after sentencing, the attorneys then filed suit against anyone else who had reaped financial gain from Bob.

Our divorce settlement was a lump sum amount. I chose to make restitution to several family members and close friends from my settlement and helped others who were not clients but were in financial need. I kept a log of all the monies distributed, which I presented to the bankruptcy attorneys. I did not have even close to $1,500,000, but my attorney shared that I had cooperated with the FBI and the debt was forgiven. I had to return several thousand dollars that I still had in my possession. My mother had lost an inheritance of $200,000 that was invested with Bob, so she did not have to pay the bankruptcy attorneys, nor was she ever compensated for her loss.

The legal fallout continued for several years. In 2005, I was visited at my home by a U.S. Marshal. He was investigating the validity of a verbal threat my ex-husband made in prison. He allegedly threatened to have the U.S. Attorney and the Judge who prosecuted him killed. He also alleged that my father would arrange the "hit."

He referred to my father as "Johnny Cadillac." I nearly burst out in laughter. I had never heard that nickname for my father, who was 93 years old and residing in a skilled nursing facility with late-stage dementia.

I asked my mother if she knew my father as "Johnny Cadillac," and she confirmed that he was given that nickname when he built secret storage compartments under the dashboards of Cadillacs for the mafia. This was another surreal and disturbing experience. It was hard to process that my ex-husband was threatening lives from prison and involving my father. It was equally difficult to hear about my father's further involvement with the mafia. The bad B-movie that I was living in seemed to have endless sequels.

Adoption

The following year, we planned a vacation in Mexico with my children. My mother had gifted us a timeshare week in Mexico, so we purchased plane tickets and applied for passports for my kids, who were about 6 and 8 years old at the time.

We went to the Post Office to submit the passport applications but were informed that the applications could not be accepted without written consent from their biological father. Knowing that we would not be able to obtain that consent, we left extremely disappointed. This situation also made us realize that there would be other opportunities my kids would miss out on for the rest of their minor years.

When we talked to the kids about our engagement and wedding, they expected that their last names would change along with mine. We had to explain that the only way to change their last names was through adoption.

I was a substitute teacher at their school, and they did not like that we now had different last names. These situations led to discussions about the adoption process. We consulted an adoption attorney and initiated the process. We were informed that a statute allowed for the termination of parental rights without consent if a parent was incarcerated for the majority of the child's minor years. Since they were 4 and 6 years old when their father was incarcerated and he was serving a 25-year sentence, this applied to our situation.

Understandably, my ex-husband was infuriated about the adoption and filed counter-motions from prison. It was a lengthy and challenging process, but eventually, the adoption was granted in 2004. We took the kids out of school that day and went to the courthouse for the official adoption. They were incredibly happy to have their new last names and to be a family. We then reapplied for passports and took our long-awaited family vacation in Mexico.

In 2005, the housing market was booming. I sold the house that I had lived in during my first marriage and divorce. We bought a house that had not yet been listed for sale across the street from our best friends. We were glad to be in a house that we purchased and owned as a married couple, and in a new neighborhood.

Father Issues

Both of my husbands had been estranged from their fathers for decades. They both harbored hurt and resentment from childhood, which eventually manifested in uncontrolled anger, unpredictable outbursts, and harsh, critical parenting. Children do not respond well to harsh parenting, especially if they've experienced significant trauma and loss. They often display regressive behaviors, digestive issues, behavioral problems, depression, and anxiety.

When I refused to bring my children back to the Miami facility for visits, Bob filed a motion against me from prison. Prisoners often have access to law libraries and become "armchair attorneys." I had to hire an attorney for representation in court. We went before a judge, and Bob was allowed to represent himself and cross-examine me from prison through a speakerphone. It was both a disturbing and bizarre experience.

He was fighting for mandatory visitation and phone calls. He was not granted mandatory visitation, which would have been a significant issue when he was transferred to prisons out of state. However, he was granted mandatory phone calls three days per week. I had to accept phone charges for the calls and was not permitted to listen in on the calls with my then 5- and 7-year-olds. Apparently, listening in on calls with young children is considered a felony.

Back then, we had a landline and were able to have two different phone numbers and ringtones. The kids liked talking to their father until they began to mention Harry's name and the upcoming wedding. His tone would change with them, becoming angrier and harsher. Both kids began showing regressive behaviors like bedwetting, sleeping in my bed, and stomach aches. The ringtone became a trigger, and at times, they would choose not to answer his call. I refused to force them to talk to him.

Soon after Harry and I married and he moved in with us, his angry outbursts began. I remember walking into the house through the garage door one day and seeing him picking up the kids' shoes and throwing them everywhere in a rage. In that moment, I remember thinking to myself, "Oh no, what have I done? I can't live with a rager again, but my kids have just been through a divorce."

Those rages continued throughout our marriage and worsened under the influence of alcohol. He refused to take ownership of his unpredictable, angry outbursts or to apologize for his intimidating behaviors.

Harry was an exceptionally clean eater and a triathlete, so our pantry and diets were completely overhauled when he moved in after the wedding. My son was having upper respiratory issues and had just been diagnosed with asthma. The asthma specialist prescribed a regimen of medication, inhalers, and OTC allergy tablets. At Harry's suggestion, we removed dairy products from our diets, and my son's symptoms disappeared. He never needed the prescribed medications.

The health of both children improved so dramatically that our pediatrician even commented on the absence of sick visits and only routine annual check-ups. They did receive required vaccinations for school, but knowing what I know now, I would have refused.

My son was very athletic and preferred to eat healthier foods. My daughter was also athletic but, like me, enjoyed sugar and carbs over vegetables. Harry would criticize her food choices daily, causing her much shame and anxiety and eventually leading to rebellion. The more critical he was of her food choices and her grades in school, the more anxiety she experienced. He refused to listen to my requests to stop being harsh and critical.

I found a male counselor, and we tried family counseling and marital counseling. Harry would not allow the focus to be on him or accept constructive feedback from the counselor. He eventually stormed out of a session and refused to return.

As with my first marriage, I chose to ignore all red flags and the warnings of close friends. The false belief that I played over and over in my mind was that no man would want to marry a 37-year-old, divorced mother of two young children whose ex-husband was in federal prison. The fact that Harry pursued a relationship with me even under these circumstances led me to ignore all serious concerns and remarry too quickly. Additionally, he didn't have biological children, and my children didn't have their father present, so it seemed like a perfect match.

Couch to Couch: In my private practice, I observed a trend twice a year where I would be contacted by past, current, and new clients to schedule sessions.

The first influx of clients would be from April to June. Most of the presenting issues involved families-of-origin, particularly mothers and fathers.

In April, families would get together for Easter and Passover. In May, families would honor mothers and grandmothers on Mother's Day. In June, families would honor fathers and grandfathers on Father's Day. For individuals or couples that had conflictual relationships with or were estranged from family members, or had lost a parent or significant family member, these holidays triggered unresolved emotions and grief reactions.

The second influx of clients was from October to December. Families have expectations for Halloween, Thanksgiving, Christmas, and Hanukkah. They may also have painful memories connected to these holidays, birthdays, and anniversaries that trigger unresolved grief and intense emotions.

Practical Application: Although clients would present with seemingly unrelated issues, the triggers were often rooted in unhealed wounds from parents or significant family members. Sadly, these family dynamics are unconsciously repeated from generation to generation.

The therapy process of healing painful memories, grieving losses, and choosing to forgive is one highly effective way to end dysfunctional family patterns.

Even if family members are unwilling to reconcile relationships, we can change family dynamics for our children and future generations.

"He's My Brother"

I planned a surprise 70th birthday party for my mother in our neighborhood clubhouse. It was a wonderful celebration with family and friends. I held the party about a month before her birthday to make it a surprise.

My mother's actual 70th birthday was in August 2005. She was back in NY so we called to wish her a joyful day on the way to school in the morning. A few hours later, I received a call from my mother and brother. My brother was in the hospital for gall bladder surgery and had just been diagnosed with pancreatic cancer. I knew little about pancreatic cancer, but I did know that it was extremely aggressive. His cancer had progressed too far, and he was too weak for chemotherapy or radiation treatments.

Two weeks later, my half-sister was diagnosed with breast cancer. She underwent surgery and chemotherapy, and the cancer was removed. Our father was in a nursing home at that time as well. I flew to NY and visited my father in the nursing home, then my sister in one hospital and my brother in another hospital.

Each time my brother was hospitalized over the next few months, I would fly to NY and stay with him. The nurses would provide a reclining chair for me to sleep in since nights were difficult when pain and fear would peak for him.

On Christmas Day in 2005, my children and I flew to NY to celebrate with our family. When we landed, I was informed that my brother's health was rapidly declining. My children went with family members to my cousin's house, and I went with my brother to the hospital by ambulance. When I returned home to Florida, I wrote the following journal entries:

Christmas Day 2005 was a day of journeys—a flight from West Palm Beach to New York followed by an ambulance ride with my brother to the trauma center at the local hospital. As his Health Care Surrogate, I was asked to sign a DNR (Do Not Resuscitate) order in accordance with his wishes. My emotions took their own journey, from the anticipated joy of being with family for the holidays to the bittersweet anticipation of seeing my brother. This was mixed with the disappointment of knowing he was not well enough to spend Christmas Day with our family, and then the unexplainable deep sadness as hospital staff attempted to "prepare" family members for his imminent death.

Inoperable pancreatic cancer, septic shock, and labored breathing are all frightening medical occurrences, but I found myself most disturbed by the paralyzing fear of my relatives. Our mother denied the existence of a living will to the paramedics, tried to refuse the DNR order desired by her son, and interfered with the administering of pain medication to make him comfortable because of the possible effects on his already labored breathing. As a mother myself, I truly cannot imagine the depth of pain and grief experienced in watching your child suffer through a terminal illness. Worse yet would be to go through such a trial without faith for comfort and with a terrifying fear of death and the unknown after death.

My mother and I slept in my brother's hospital room with him for the first two nights. I watched as she furiously attempted to take every measure possible to prolong his life (and unfortunately, his suffering). When he was more alert and responsive, he asked for pain medication, and she argued with him against it until the hospital staff intervened and responded to his request (he was 54 years old at that time). In his Living Will, he refused extraordinary measures and only desired to be comfortable and to die with dignity.

And so, my brother hung on with the assistance of full oxygen, four intravenous antibiotics, intravenous nutrition, an external bag draining his liver, catheterization, a central line in his thigh, a medicated dressing for a Stage 2 bedsore, a medication patch, and a port in his arm when there were no longer veins available for drawing blood. He was not able to get out of bed on his own; sitting in a chair with the assistance of male staff was exhausting. He could barely take in clear liquids without severe nausea and incontinence, had blood clots in his leg, and a feeding tube for "severe malnutrition," according to his oncologist. He rarely complained about his physical pain but was terribly distressed about the incontinence and felt very depressed and fearful.

He began moaning in his sleep and seemed haunted by his dreams. He tearfully wished he could go to sleep and wake up with a new body. When I delicately suggested that someday we all would have a new body in heaven, he avoided any further discussion. I wondered how anyone could look death in the eye without the hope of taking Jesus' hand and spending forever with Him in heaven. The incomprehensible fear of the unknown when we leave our physical body was too much to bear for my brother. When he awoke terrified in the early morning hours, I could only hold his hands tightly, hold him close to me, and cry with him, trying desperately to comfort him but unable to give him the only Hope I know to be true if he wasn't willing to receive it.

I watched as family members, close friends, and even hospital staff offered their own personal sources of hope to him—holy water from monks for him to drink, medals with saints' names and pictures on them, and sepulchers holding religious relics placed around his neck. They believed that these religious objects and rituals held the power to heal him. Yet, some of the same family members were concerned about me bringing a statue of Jesus carrying a man, "Footprints in the Sand," that I was giving him as a gift. The only true source of Hope was not invited into that desperately hopeless and fearful hospital room.

In this very uncertain season of life, I can be certain of this: No Jesus. No peace. Know Jesus. Know peace.

We extended our five-day visit to ten days in order to celebrate the New Year with my brother and mother. I tried to make it a special day for my extended family members and my children. My children had never seen snow. As we pulled out of the parking lot in the morning, it began snowing, and they were so excited. We visited Grandpa at the nursing home and pushed him around in his wheelchair. Although he no longer knows who we are, at 93 years old, he is still physically healthy and enjoyed our visit. We then visited my sister and her husband. She completed her chemotherapy treatments the week before Christmas and looked wonderful.

My sister and her husband greeted us in their professional clown costumes, performed a show for my kids, made balloon flowers and animals, and face-painted my 8-year-old daughter. After our visit and more snow outside, we went to the hospital with a bouquet of flower balloons, a face-painted Dalmatian little girl, a portable DVD player, "The Polar Express" (my brother's request), and NYE hats and blowers. My brother was so excited to see all of us. We watched the movie together and enjoyed every moment with him.

When my brother was in the trauma room, the physician-on-call and nursing staff were preparing us for the very real possibility that he would not live through the night. Amazingly, as each day passed, he grew stronger and responded to the treatment administered. I believe that had he still been at home without this medical intervention, we would not have had the gift of each extra day with him. My children were given an extra two weeks with their favorite uncle.

It may not have been as I planned for that Christmas, but I can see now that God's plan was beyond my understanding and exceeded our family's plans.

Three days later, we returned to Florida. I never imagined it would be my children's last visit with Uncle John and that I would return in less than three weeks. This was really hard to understand since a feeding tube was inserted into his abdomen and his oncologist believed that his strength would be restored within 2-3 weeks.

My brother had decided during the previous visit that he wanted to give up his apartment and come to Florida to stay in my home. We were planning to rent an RV to transport him from the hospital to my home. I was able to find a company that had a store in the same town as my uncle, who was close to my brother. He had offered to drive the RV, and we could return it near my home. My mother, with the help of family and friends, packed all of his belongings and hired movers to transport them all to Florida.

And once again, it appeared that he would not live through the night. Early Sunday morning, his body rejected the feeding tube and water. He was already severely malnourished, his body filled with fluid (referred to as third spacing), he still battled sepsis and a severe bedsore, his body began leaking fluids through his skin (an odor that is not easily forgotten), his breathing was extremely labored due to fluid in the lungs, he was on 100% oxygen from a mask, and he moaned in agony whenever he was moved. He was less responsive every day that passed, and he was not able to either focus his eyes or even close his eyes for days. Then, the medical decisions became even more difficult, and the "Why, God?" questions more frequent.

I asked God why my brother, my only safe person, was dying. Why did he have to suffer hour after hour and day after day? Why did I have to make life-and-death decisions daily and even hourly on my brother's behalf? It was all too much and the most painful loss that I have ever experienced.

In my brother's Living Will, he refused all extraordinary measures to prolong life. His only request was to be made comfortable with medication. This meant I had to refuse a respirator, refuse a surgical procedure to reinsert the feeding tube (which would neither improve nor reverse his condition), and I had to refuse intravenous nutrients (which would add unnecessary fluids to his body) on my brother's behalf. We were told that these measures are offered to the family solely for the comfort of the family and that they would not improve my brother's condition.

The even more difficult decision was to administer a morphine drip to make him comfortable, knowing that it would depress his already labored breathing and hasten the dying process. I was watching my brother drown in his own fluids, starving from an inability for his body to absorb nutrients, and suffering with no way to communicate except by moaning in constant pain. I wanted his suffering to end, but I knew that although the morphine would medicate the pain, it would also inevitably stop his breathing. Either way, he was dying, and his pain and my pain of losing him were unbearable.

On the sixth night that I slept at the hospital, the morphine reached a dosage level that allowed my brother's eyes to close and his breathing to seem less labored. My mother, our uncle, and I slept in his hospital room in chairs.

Amazingly, it was peaceful through the night, and at 5:20 AM on January 26, 2006, it was as though God gently woke me up. I remember looking at my brother to be sure he was still breathing. Within minutes, my uncle woke up, and I silently gestured to him to join me at my brother's bedside. I leaned close to my brother and spoke to him, and then we watched as he peacefully took his last breath. My mother woke up, and we began to comfort her as she realized that her son was no longer breathing and experienced a mother's indescribable sorrow and pain.

Although those final six days in the hospital room with my brother were extremely difficult, they allowed me to learn more about him and the lives that he deeply impacted. Each hour of each day brought different family members, friends, neighbors, church members, and even hospital staff with beautiful stories of how he touched their lives. He had a gift for making people feel special and making them laugh. Visitors would stay for hours, holding his hand, talking to him even when he was not able to respond, sharing stories and pictures from his life (especially his group of lifelong friends), laughing, and then crying, knowing this precious man would soon leave us.

We were blessed to personally know the Nursing Supervisor who is a family friend. She later told me that in all her years in nursing, she had never experienced such a transformation in her staff as with my brother. They were deeply impacted by him and moved to a level of compassion that she was not able to teach.

Almost everyone that my brother met was drawn to him. He had a great capacity to love, to make friends and strangers alike feel special, to sacrifice his own needs and comfort for others, to forgive and choose peace over hate, and to desire reconciliation and restoration of relationships in his work and everyday life. I find great comfort in knowing that God measures a man not by his outward appearance (or wealth, profession, house, car) but by his heart. My brother's heart for his family, his friends, and everyone he encountered was immeasurable. I miss him terribly, but I am so grateful to have had him for my brother.

When I was young, the song "He Ain't Heavy, He's My Brother," written by Bobby Scott and Bob Russell came out and I would sing it to him. During his last months of life, the lyrics were even more meaningful:

His welfare is my concern, no burden is he to bear. . .
And the load, doesn't weigh me down at all
He ain't heavy, he's my brother.

Reconnection

The following year, on January 7, 2007, my father passed away. My half-siblings and I arranged for a military service and burial at a cemetery on Long Island. Several uniformed men played "Taps," folded the American flag, and unexpectedly presented it to me at my siblings' request. That gesture impacted me deeply.

Over the next few years, my marriage was struggling. I searched for a male counselor, hoping my husband would feel more comfortable with a male rather than a female counselor, since he was already married to one. We attended individual, marital, and family sessions. Unfortunately, he denied his damaging behaviors and patterns. We separated for several months in 2009, but then we prematurely reunited. His destructive patterns gradually resurfaced since he never acknowledged and owned them. In 2010, we sold our house and moved into separate homes.

Harry and I remained separated from 2010 until March 2016, when our divorce was finalized. We tried mediation twice, but ultimately had to hire attorneys and were required to have a third mediation. He was dating and in a committed relationship by 2012. They married after the divorce was finalized.

In her early teen years, my daughter began asking about her paternal grandmother and her father. She decided to reach out to her Nana by phone after many years of no contact. Several months later, we made plans to meet in Arkansas where their father was incarcerated. I also allowed my daughter to read newspaper articles that explained why their father was arrested and indicted.

In 2011, I flew with both kids to Arkansas to see both their nana and father. I had to escort them for the visit to the prison since they were minors. I remember all the visitors were lined up against a wall in a large room with plastic chairs, tables, and vending machines. The opposite wall had three full-length murals. One mural depicted Marvel characters, another featured Disney princesses, and the third displayed a Thomas Kinkade painting with angels. Bob had painted similar Marvel and Disney murals on the walls in our kids' playroom. The three of us looked at the murals and immediately recognized his style.

He was overjoyed to see both kids, and they each had some alone time with him for more intimate visits. Their Nana was also incredibly happy to be reunited with her grandchildren.

The following year, I drove the kids to Arkansas to visit their father again. We then drove to Georgia and stayed with their Nana for several days. Both visits were difficult for me since the wounds of deception and betrayal were reopened by ongoing lies. Nevertheless, I knew my kids needed to reconnect with their father and grandmother.

One Saturday evening in 2012, I was watching the television show "Who the Bleep Did I Marry?" on Discovery ID. At the end of the show, there was a message inviting viewers to email personal stories of being blindsided in a marriage. I emailed a brief summary of my story, never expecting a response.

On Monday morning, I received a phone call from the Assistant Producer of the show. At first, I thought it was a scam call, but she mentioned the name of the show and referred to my email submission. She explained that the show's intention was to raise awareness of red flags in relationships in the hopes of preventing destructive relationships. I was forced to be silent about my story for a decade, but this show presented an opportunity for me to speak up and hopefully raise awareness among women stuck in toxic relationships.

The crew came to Florida and filmed the episode over a weekend. We filmed at my friend's house in PGA National. It was emotionally and physically draining, but very cathartic and freeing to tell my story. The show aired in March 2013. Season 5, Episode 9 was called "Marvelous Deception." I believe the show was helpful to a small population that watched as well as to my clients who knew my story.

Bob was transferred to Miami before his release in May 2020. He was released two years early due to the pandemic. My son was visiting from California to celebrate his sister's birthday and college graduation. They found out their father would be released the day my son was leaving, so we extended his trip.

My son picked up his father in Miami upon his release. He took him shopping for clothes and shoes, then treated him to several meals. My daughter joined them for the drive to Georgia, where he would be living. They lovingly and willingly offered to pick him up, provide for his basic needs, and drive him out of state as an act of honoring their father. I'm immensely proud of both of them.

Couch to Couch: In my years as a therapist, I've observed that it is more common for teen girls than boys to seek out their biological parents if they were separated from them or adopted at birth. It's an innate desire that seems to be wired into them. Girls especially want to know their fathers which often leads to finding their Heavenly Father.

Forgiveness

In 2016, my mother admitted that she could no longer live alone, even with part-time caretakers. She wanted me to purchase a single-family home in the community where I was renting. I bought a house, packed and sold her condo, packed my townhouse, and moved us in within 60 days.

My mother, daughter, and I moved into our new home in June 2016. My son was living in the college dorms in Tallahassee. He moved to California the following summer for a career opportunity in the solar energy industry. It was difficult knowing he would be so far away, but I vowed I would encourage my kids to pursue new endeavors even when it meant leaving the nest.

My mother was very dependent on caretakers while I was working, then on me and my daughter the rest of the time. She was starting to show signs of dementia and would become verbally aggressive toward us. She also battled depression and anxiety for many years and developed Tardive Dyskinesia (TD) from prolonged use of psychotropic medications. The TD caused involuntary movements of her mouth and jaw, which was very distressing to her.

These were some of the most emotionally challenging years of my adulthood. My mother had been emotionally dependent on me since childhood. There was a role reversal throughout my life, and in the final months of her life, she even referred to me as her mother.

I was also a pseudo-spouse during my childhood. This is a common dynamic with single mothers. Sons are often put into the husband or "man of the house" role, especially if the husband died or abandoned the family. My brother played this role when my mother was in NY. I played the role when she moved to Florida and after he passed.

I stored a lot of hurt, anger, and resentment toward my mother over the years. It began surfacing daily when we lived together. I went through years of my own insight therapy and thought I had forgiven her. I learned that forgiveness is not a one-time, all-encompassing decision. Over the course of the next year, I wrote down every hurt and offense I was holding against my mother from childhood through adulthood.

Dementia also brought paranoid and accusatory thinking on my mother's part. She was verbally aggressive and hurtful toward me and my daughter even though we were her primary caregivers. I continued writing down each offense. I would find alone time to ask God to help me forgive each offense one by one.

I know I am limited in my capacity to love those who are unlovable and to completely forgive over and over again. God expanded my capacity to love and forgive. I also know that God loved me when I was most unlovable and has forgiven me many times over.

I clearly remember pulling into my driveway after work one evening and feeling a tremendous sense of freedom and peace. I had finally released and forgiven years of hurt and resentment that I had stored deep down inside.

The final six months of my mother's life were vastly different. I no longer felt hurt or offended by her words. I felt a much deeper compassion toward her. I know that she was emotionally neglected as a child, then abandoned by her father. She was a wounded little girl inside an adult woman's body desperately seeking to be loved and nurtured.

My mother did not lean on faith in God during her adulthood. Following surgery in October 2017 and still groggy from anesthesia, she told me that Jesus was at the door to her ICU room. She described Him as wearing a white garment with a belt and sandals. Jesus told her He would come back for her.

Seven months later, on May 20, 2018, she was surrounded by family when she peacefully took her last breath. Shortly before that, I whispered in her ear that when she was ready, to call out to Jesus, and He would come back for her. I believe she did, and that He took her hand as He promised.

Couch to Couch: Before my mother passed, I asked God to help me forgive her for the hurt and emotional wounds that had never healed. I've learned that hurt from wounds that are never addressed and forgiven, turn into resentment and roots of bitterness. Unforgiveness is poison to our hearts, minds, and bodies.

I've witnessed wounded adult children anxiously waiting to hear an apology or acknowledgment of wrongdoings from a parent on their deathbed. Once they pass, the adult children are left devastated knowing they will never again have the opportunity to hear that parent express remorse and ask forgiveness.

They either remain resentful and bitter or try to deny their pain by idealizing the memory of their parent. These adults tend to never properly grieve by keeping all the damaging emotions inside, and eventually have mental and physical health issues.

**Forgiveness is extremely important,
particularly with aging parents and family members**.

Practical Application:

❖ Forgiveness only requires one person – YOU!
❖ Forgiveness does not have to directly involve the person you are forgiving.
❖ Choose to forgive while they are still alive.
❖ Choose to forgive even if you never receive an apology.
❖ Even if you don't reconcile with the person you are forgiving, you will benefit from letting go of the hurt and resentment and releasing them.
❖ Forgiveness is a personal heart matter that God will lovingly help you with if you just ask.
❖ List each hurt and offense, then ask God to help you forgive one by one.

Choose forgiveness.
You will experience a freedom and peace that is indescribable.

Serial Weight Cycler

My lifelong, self-destructive pattern of yo-yo dieting peaked when my mother lived with me. I am admittedly a Serial Weight Cycler - a person who follows a predictable behavior pattern of losing and regaining weight repeatedly (I personally created this label and definition).

As a young child, I definitely concluded that food is safe, comforting, and dependable, unlike the significant adults in my life. Sweets filled the void of abandonment and rejection and provided comfort when grieving losses. Food, particularly sweets, has been my drug of choice throughout my life and continues to be a daily battle.

Several relatives died when I was young. I was brought to funeral homes without any understanding of death and the grieving process. Adults would be crying and deeply grieved, then go out to dinner between viewings. After the burial, there was always a large dinner at a restaurant. I silently observed that painful feelings are not talked about, but instead food serves as a source of comfort when grieving a loss.

Weight loss became exponentially more difficult with pregnancies, divorces, significant losses, hormonal imbalances, and menopause. As a counselor and in my adult life, I've noticed that many women lose their appetite and lose weight when experiencing divorce and other losses. I'm part of the minority of women who gain weight when feeling trapped in a relationship or situation, through divorce, and when deeply grieving significant losses.

Recently, I decided to compile a list of diets, food plans, exercise programs, natural supplements, workbooks, and Bible studies that I have tried over the past 35 years to lose weight and maintain a healthier lifestyle. I'm ashamed to admit that there are over seventy different methods on that list. That is an average of two methods per year for 35 years.

In 2017, I wrote the following journal entry. I was attempting to acknowledge my food addiction and to identify the stored emotions and negative core beliefs that fueled this addiction:

Dear addiction to food,

Although this has been a lifelong relationship, I need to end this for the last time.

I realize you were with me throughout my childhood, teen years, and adulthood, through many traumas and losses, through deaths and divorces, and all kinds of setbacks. You were faithfully always there when my mother was unable to meet my emotional needs, and when my father was physically and emotionally absent for most of my life.

When staying at my grandmother's house was uncomfortable and fearful, you were Carvel ice cream, Good Humor ice cream, canned peaches and ice cream, and Rice Krispie treats.

I think you were withheld from me at times. I had to ask permission to get to you; at other times, you were readily available at my first job in the bakery—all sugar and flour products—chocolate horns, black-n-white cookies, chocolate-dipped sprinkle cookies.

When I moved to Florida and lived on my own, you were scarce due to lack of finances until I started to work at Savannah's Hospital and then met my first husband. He fed us both a lot! Jupiter Crab Company most nights after work on Singer Island, with butter-drenched breadsticks. I stuffed myself during both pregnancies—60 lb. weight gain each one—probably terrified of staying trapped in my marriage and being a mother of two children.

When I was a single mother, you were with me, and now I had the resources to buy all the food I wanted to fill my emptiness, loneliness, fear, and anxiety.

In my second marriage, I was again restricted from accessing you. When he would go on shift, I would be with you secretly—Oreo cookies, sprinkles, Girl Scout cookies. And then when my brother was in the hospital and I felt so alone, you were there—French vanilla coffees, pizza, Entenmann's cakes. And when he died, I gained 40 lbs.

The worst weight gain has been the past 2 years as my mother's physical and emotional needs have increased, as well as her emotional and physical dependence on me. She has not been able or willing to put herself and her own needs aside at all, and instead depends on me and my daughter.

So, just as in the beginning of my life and during childhood, I seek to meet my own emotional needs with food, to medicate fear, anxiety, frustration, resentment, loneliness, and feeling trapped, and to gain a sense of control over her and my circumstances by controlling her food intake and my own—sugar and flour especially. I don't even recognize this body as my own when I look in the mirror.

I have to end my dependence on food to meet my emotional needs and medicate my emotional pain, fear, and anxiety. I have to divorce you, completely sever my dysfunctional relationship that I am trapped in, and now, trapped inside this large body. I have to end my affair with sugar and flour or it will end me!

I will not starve to death. I will not die. I will not become severely depressed or unable to function and work.

I will be okay. I will feel better. I will look healthy and fit. I will fit in all of my clothes, and I will be more attractive.

God, my Father, will sustain me, fill me, heal me. He will restore my body to a healthy size and state and will replenish all that was stolen emotionally throughout my life, especially by my mother. I will no longer be trapped inside this fat. I will be free!

Good-bye dependence on food!!! Forever!

I'm determined to end the serial weight cycling before I begin the next decade of my life. I reached my peak weight in 2019. I've made significant changes in my diet over the past four years: eliminating caffeine (coffee, green tea, matcha tea, dark chocolate) and refined sugar products; focusing on organic, no antibiotics/no steroids added poultry or beef, and fresh vegetables; avoiding pork products (for Biblical reasons and due to high parasitic content) and abstaining from shellfish (for Biblical reasons and because they are considered vacuums of the sea floor).

I am currently down 50 lbs. and three sizes. I purchased a beautiful light blue Calvin Klein suit at the beginning of the pandemic. Shopping was almost exclusively online and this suit was discounted 60%. The only problem was that they did not have my size. I purchased the size they had and patiently waited four years to fit in it. I was able to proudly wear that suit to an event last month. I'm close to my goal of losing 60 lbs. by my 60th birthday this summer!

Couch to Couch: I remember a research study from Psychology 101 in college. The results highlighted the importance of **emotional needs** being met in infants in order for them to thrive.

In the early 1900's, orphanages had alarmingly high death rates. This was blamed on contagious diseases, so attempts were made to keep orphanages sterile and to isolate children from each other.

Austrian psychoanalyst and physician Rene Spitz proposed an alternate theory. He thought that infants in institutions were missing important parental relationships and suffered from lack of being held, nurtured, and loved.

To test his theory, he compared a group of infants raised in isolated orphanage cribs with those raised in prison with their mothers. If the germs from being locked up in an unsterile setting were the problem, the infants in the prison would have done poorly.

The results proved his theory: 37% of the infants kept in the orphanage died, but there were no deaths among the infants raised in the prison. The orphans who managed to survive were more likely to contract all types of illnesses. They were underweight and showed psychological, cognitive, and behavioral deficits. In contrast, the incarcerated babies grew more quickly, were larger, and did better in every way Spitz could measure.

I've shared this study with many clients to highlight the crucial importance of having **emotional needs** met not only during childhood but well into adulthood.

Practical Application: Children unconsciously equate eating with a parent's attention and nurturance. When **emotional needs** are neglected or ignored, children may overeat throughout their life in the hope of having their needs finally met. Often, the more obese a person is, the more emotionally starved they were at some significant stage in their life.

To address these unmet **emotional needs** in constructive and fulfilling ways, integrate these strategies into your life:

- ❖ **Seek Professional Counseling**: A therapist can help you understand and process your emotional needs.
- ❖ **Build Strong Relationships**: Connect with friends and family who offer support, understanding, and companionship.
- ❖ **Join Support Groups**: Participate in groups where you can share experiences and gain support from others facing similar challenges.
- ❖ **Develop a Self-Care Routine**: Nurture yourself with relaxing baths, massage therapy, reading or spending time in nature.

Growing Faith

The question I've most commonly been asked over the past 20 years is, "How did you get through all of that?" I love that question because I enjoy sharing my faith and giving God all the credit for keeping me and my children alive and thriving.

As I look back on my entire life from infancy through adulthood, I'm able to connect the dots of spiritual warfare. Spiritual warfare refers to the concept of a battle or conflict that occurs on a spiritual level between forces of good and evil. This battle is believed to take place in the invisible realm, beyond what we can see with our physical eyes.

The forces of good are often associated with God and His Holy Spirit, while the forces of evil are associated with Satan and demonic spirits. God creates. Satan counterfeits and destroys.

During my early childhood, I would often have nightmares. There were nights when I would feel the physical presence of a spiritual entity next to me in bed or standing in my bedroom. In the context of spiritual warfare, nightmares are interpreted as a manifestation of the battle between good and evil forces. It is believed that evil spirits or entities may use nightmares as a way to gain access to an individual's mind and sow seeds of fear, doubt, and negativity.

Sleep paralysis is often associated with spiritual warfare as well. Sleep paralysis is a condition where an individual experiences a temporary inability to move or speak while falling asleep or waking up. I've had many nightmares where I'm trying to run and can't move, trying to call for help and can't speak, and even trying to sit up or wake up but feel paralyzed. Sleep paralysis can be accompanied by vivid and frightening hallucinations, which can cause feelings of fear, panic, and helplessness.

As an adult, my friends suggested I call out the name of "Jesus" during these nightmares. It would take several very distorted tries for my voice to be free to utter His name, but it worked. The nightmares would stop immediately, and I would wake up. They referenced the verse in Luke 10:17, "Lord, even the demons are subject to us in your name!"

Several months after marital separation in 1999, I went to a retreat in Georgia called "Healing for the Nations." One evening during chapel service, I experienced a spiritual attack or demonic oppression. I felt a presence holding me down. I was overcome with fear and started crying. There were prayer counselors in the room. They surrounded me and prayed against these spirits. The attack immediately stopped. Not only did the fear subside, but I experienced amazing inner peace. This was my first experience with deliverance.

Deliverance refers to the act of being set free from bondage or oppression by evil spirits or negative energies. It is often associated with religious or spiritual practices and is believed to involve the expulsion or removal of these harmful influences from an individual's life. It is not exorcism as often portrayed in movies.

Deliverance from ancestral demons refers to the process of being set free from the influence of evil spirits that are believed to be inherited from one's ancestors. There is a related concept of generational curses where negative patterns or behaviors (addictions, mental illnesses, physical illnesses, divorce) are passed down from one generation to the next.

The day after my first deliverance experience, an older woman at the retreat asked me if I was ever involved in occult practices. At first, I responded "no" because I thought she was asking if I was ever a member of a cult. When I asked her what she meant, she provided me with a list of occult practices that can open spiritual doors for evil spirits to oppress us. These were practices that I innocently and unknowingly was introduced to by peers and family members:

- Ouija Board
- Black Magic
- Levitation
- Fortune-telling
- Horoscopes
- Seances
- Channeling
- Crystals
- Magic Eight Ball
- Horror movies
- Dream Catchers
- Sweat Lodges
- Peace Pipe Ceremonies

In 2013, I was introduced to a woman whose ministry was prayer and deliverance. We met for several days, and she walked me through each stage of my life from birth to the present, addressing emotional wounds, ancestral demons, generational curses, occult practices, doors opened for evil spirits to attack and oppress, and unforgiveness in my heart. On the last day, I asked her about being "baptized in the Holy Spirit."

"Baptized in the Holy Spirit" is a term used by many Christian denominations to describe a profound experience of the Holy Spirit's presence and power in a person's life. The experience of being baptized in the Holy Spirit is believed to result in a deepening of one's relationship with God, a greater sense of spiritual empowerment, and a closer alignment with the will of God. It is often described as a feeling of being filled with the Holy Spirit, with evidence of speaking in tongues or other spiritual gifts.

The deliverance counselor began praying for me. I experienced a demonic attack where I couldn't speak and was overwhelmed with fear. She repeatedly asked the demon that was attacking me its name, and finally, I was able to speak a name aloud. She commanded the spirit to leave me alone. The attack stopped, and I felt calm and peaceful. She continued to pray, and I was filled with the Holy Spirit and began speaking in tongues, specifically in Hebrew.

I was not familiar with Hebrew and had never spoken Hebrew. I spoke the Hebrew name of Jesus, which is Yahusha HaMaschiach. We actually Googled the name since neither of us had ever heard it before.

I've learned that God and Lord are titles, not the true Biblical names for our Creator. The correct Hebrew name is Yahuah. When we say HalleluYah, we are praising His name, Yah.

I had been attending Christian churches for twenty years. I attended several small groups over those years but was most comfortable participating in women's Bible study groups. In

2014, a friend of mine invited me to her women's group. The women in this group were studying the Biblical Hebrew roots of our faith and the Hebrew language in which the earliest scriptures were penned.

Our group leaders had learned that many Christians and Jews around the world have been studying the original Hebrew and the entire Bible—the Old and New Testaments. They are learning and following Torah (the first five books of the Bible), as well as believing that Yahusha (Jesus) is the Son of Yahuah (God), our Messiah and Savior, who died in our place and was resurrected.

We learned that all of the 40,000 Christian denominations that exist globally today were ultimately birthed out of the Catholic Church. The Roman Emperor Constantine changed the Sabbath from the 7th day of the week to the 1st day of the week, Sunday.

The Biblical Feast Days were forbidden by the early church, even though Jesus observed them and God tells us to observe them "forever throughout your generations." (Leviticus 23) The Catholic church replaced the Feast Days with Easter and Christmas. Biblical scholars know that Jesus was not born on December 25th, and yet this is the day the church continues to celebrate his birth. In fact, it was a customary practice to celebrate the birth of numerous pagan gods on December 25th.

The seven Biblical Feast Days are:

- Feast of Passover
- Feast of Unleavened Bread
- Feast of Firstfruits
- Feast of the Harvest (Shavuot)
- Feast of Trumpets (Yom Teruah)
- Day of Atonement (Yom Kippur)
- Feast of Tabernacles (Sukkot)

These Feast Days are very meaningful and commemorate key events in Biblical history, such as the Exodus of the Israelites from slavery in Egypt (Passover) and the giving of the Torah (Ten Commandments) on Mount Sinai (Shavuot). They also reaffirm our faith in and dedication to Our Creator.

As I stated before, God creates, and Satan counterfeits. Satan even counterfeited Creation with Evolution Theory. It makes sense that he would attack theology and steer Bible translations. He wants humans to worship him and not Yahuah.

Sadly, the women in our group attended various churches and the pastors of our churches were not willing to hear about what we were learning. We were even told that these were false teachings and that we had strayed away from our faith. On the contrary, our understanding of God and His Word grew even deeper.

One night, I had a very vivid dream where I could feel Jesus next to me. My head was tilted back and it seemed like he was pouring water on my head as if to wash my hair. It was the most serene, peaceful dream I have ever experienced.

When I told my women's group about the dream, the leader suggested that I was being anointed with oil, as in Psalm 23:5, "You anoint my head with oil; my cup overflows." In the Old Testament, being anointed with oil signifies being set apart for a specific purpose or role. My heart's desire is to fulfill whatever purpose God has for my life as He rewrites my story.

Reinventing Myself

The rewriting of my story has begun. It has been a transformative journey involving insight therapy, deliverance counseling, a deeper understanding of my faith, and a holistic lifestyle. The survival chapters have been followed by chapters of healing, growth, and new beginnings. Rewriting is a continual process throughout our lives.

When the pandemic began in early 2020, I was experiencing career burnout after 30 years as a psychotherapist. Finances were very tight, and I was unable to keep up with mortgage payments. I had even rented out a room to supplement my income.

I refused to accept the midlife crisis label; I was determined to experience a midlife makeover instead. I began having Zoom calls with my aunt and cousins in Indiana and Illinois. We were all genuinely concerned about the pandemic, civil unrest, and political turmoil in our country.

My aunt was living alone since her husband was in a nursing home. My cousins suggested selling my home and moving to Indiana. Initially, I could live with my aunt and apply for a position at the hospital where my cousin worked in Illinois.

I listed my house with a realtor in July, and it was under contract in one week. I continued scheduling telehealth sessions with clients while systematically cleaning out my home. My side business as a Professional Organizer equipped me for the enormous task of emptying a house—furniture, household items, wall hangings, memorabilia, and outdated personal and professional documents. A few boxes were shipped to Indiana, and the remaining minimal necessities were packed into my car for the move.

I applied for professional licensure in both Indiana and Illinois. The Indiana license allowed me to continue telehealth sessions with my Florida clients. I was hired by the hospital in Illinois where my cousin worked.

The house closing was during the first week of October. Two weeks later, I was on the road to my next chapter. God showed me my next assignment during that long drive. I had a sense that while working at the hospital, I would minister to the ICU nurses overwhelmed with COVID patients and deaths.

A few months later, the Director of Nursing inquired if there was a social worker on staff with a strong faith who would be interested in co-facilitating a workshop for ICU nurses. My director asked if I was interested. I gladly accepted the assignment and was able to co-facilitate workshops on "Finding Meaning in a Year of Crisis."

The Nursing Director referenced two Bible verses in her PowerPoint presentation. The first verse was Genesis 22:1, "After these things, God tested Abraham, and said to him, 'Abraham!' And he said, 'Here I am.'" Abraham was obedient to God to go wherever He led him.

The second verse referenced in the workshop was Esther 4:14, "And who knows whether you have not come to the kingdom for such a time as this?" This has been a very meaningful and affirming verse for me over the past twenty years.

I enjoyed spending time with my aunt while living with her in Indiana. I also spent time with my youngest cousin and assisted her on a professional organizing job in Chicago. That was much less stressful and more enjoyable work than the hospital position.

By the summer of 2021, I was ready to move back to Florida. I appreciated my aunt lightening my financial burden by inviting me to stay with her. I was in a chronic stress state working in a hospital emergency room during a pandemic and knew I did not want to experience another northern winter. In August, I happily returned to the Sunshine State.

A therapist-turned-realtor friend had been encouraging me to become a real estate agent. While in Indiana, I enrolled in an online real estate course. I took the licensure exam when

I returned to Florida and passed. I was now a licensed psychotherapist in three states, a licensed realtor, and a professional organizer—on my way to reinventing myself.

The reinvention process began as an assistant to a Realtor and an Interior Designer. I took on several professional organizing jobs and was hired as a companion to an elderly woman when her daughter traveled.

In 2023, I transitioned my counseling practice to a life coaching program for midlife adults desiring to reinvent themselves and rewrite their story. My ReStoried® online course guides adults through the process of rewriting their personal, interpersonal, and spiritual life story.

January 2024 brought several real estate sales opportunities. I was asked to clear out and sell the 60-year home of my best friend's mother-in-law. First, I wore my professional organizer hat to empty the contents of her home. Next, I prepared the house for sale. Lastly, I guided the owner and the buyer—her grandson—through the contract to close process.

I have helped numerous family members and friends with the packing and clearing out for sale process over the past 30 years. Now, I'm assisting real estate clients with clearing out, listing, and selling their homes. My new business venture, Clear Out to Close, has been launched!

Warrior Story

The process of being ReStoried® encompasses my personal story, interpersonal story, and faith story. Regarding my personal story, I had to uncover the false self-beliefs rooted in my childhood and replace them with the truth about my value and worth. This required breaking through limiting self-beliefs and embracing self-expanding beliefs.

Rewriting my interpersonal story has been a painful yet necessary process of assessing relationships that add value or deplete value in my life. This has involved restructuring relationships, setting clear boundaries, and grieving the end of hurtful relationships.

My war story—*what I have been through*—has turned into my Warrior story—*how I got through*. As I reflect back on my life, I now know that my battles have been spiritual in nature. Through my faith in God, He has equipped me with His armor to fight. He has empowered me to be a Kingdom Warrior.

In the darkest valleys, when fear threatened to consume me, I found comfort in the words of Ephesians 6:10-17, "Finally, be strong in the Lord and in the strength of his might. Put on the full armor of God, that you may be able to stand against the schemes of the devil. For we do not wrestle against flesh and blood, but against the rulers, against the authorities, against the cosmic powers over this present darkness, against the spiritual forces of evil in the heavenly places. Therefore take up the whole armor of God, that you may be able to withstand in the evil day, having done all, to stand firm. Stand therefore, having fastened on the belt of truth, and having put on the breastplate of righteousness, and, as shoes for your feet, having put on the readiness given by the gospel of peace. In all circumstances take up the shield of faith, with which you can extinguish all the flaming darts of the evil one; and take the helmet of salvation, and the sword of the Spirit, which is the word of God, praying at all times in the Spirit, with all prayer and supplication."

My war story has indeed transformed into my Warrior story—a testament to the power of God's love and the triumph of light over darkness. As I stand amidst the ruins of the battlefield, I know that the scars of war are gentle reminders of the grace that carried me through. I was never alone in the battles. My Heavenly Father always fought for me and right beside me.

God is still rewriting my story and will continue until I take my last breath. For now, I listen and watch for each next step in this bittersweet refining process.

My story matters. Your story matters. God has ReStoried® me. He desires to ReStory you. Trust the Author of your life story. Take up your sword and shield. Be the Kingdom Warrior you were created to be!

To purchase my online course, "ReStoried®: Transform Your Life & Rewrite Your Story in 90 Days" click on the link below or scan the QR code:

www.restoried.net

Message From The Author's Heart

I hope this book has inspired you to visit your past story, to heal your present, and to begin your new chapter.
Thank you for reading my story!

Printed in the USA
CPSIA information can be obtained
at www.ICGtesting.com
CBHW051650021024
15220CB00054B/1339